Discovering
LOST DORSET

Discovering LOST DORSET

A PERSONAL VIEW THROUGH
MAGIC LANTERN PHOTOGRAPHS AND OTHER IMAGES
OF THE COUNTY IN THE AUTHOR'S UNIQUE COLLECTION

RODNEY LEGG

DORSET BOOKS

First published in Great Britain in 2006

British Library Cataloguing-in-Publication Data
A CIP record for this title is available from the British Library

ISBN 1 871164 49 4
ISBN 978 1 871164 49 7

DORSET BOOKS
*Dorset Books is a partnership between
Dorset County Council and Halsgrove*

Halsgrove House
Lower Moor Way
Tiverton, Devon EX16 6SS
Tel: 01884 243242
Fax: 01884 243325
email: sales@halsgrove.com
website: www.halsgrove.com

Printed and bound by CPI Bath Press, Bath.

DEDICATION

*For Julie whose Chinn ancestor
is pictured within.*

INTRODUCTION

Long before I started the predecessor of *Dorset Life* magazine, in 1968, I was obsessively collecting what I call Dorsetiana. This included hoarding photographs of family and friends as well as taking my own pictures. Distant relations extended to Leggs around Puddletown and the Wareham branch of the Hardys, sharing common ancestry with Vice-Admiral Thomas Masterman Hardy of Nelson fame, and author Thomas from half a century later. Retired land-agent Charles Stride of Portland Villa, Shillingstone, contributed material from Sturminster Newton and the Blackmore Vale.

My aunt and uncle Effie and Frank Watts gave me the treasures they had inherited from George Hardy, of St Martin's Street – now North Street – in Wareham, who died on 8 March 1909. He was the brother of my paternal great-grandmother, Eliza Hardy who married John Kearley of Ridge in the Isle of Purbeck, in 1850. The metal box came via a reclusive cousin in Wareham, who was still alive between the wars, and originally included a revolver – which I last saw in the loft at The Grove in Moordown, Bournemouth – as well as souvenirs of Nelson's Hardy and HMS *Victory*.

Born on 3 July 1832, George Hardy was a baby when his eldest brother, John, was transported to Australia for theft by the same Dorchester Lent Assizes that convicted the Tolpuddle Martyrs in 1834. John Hardy's letters home from New South Wales survived, in that box, and we donated the documents to Dorset Record Office in 1966 (deposit D.681).

My father, Winton cobbler Ted Legg – born in 1902 – was given lantern slides by retired Bournemouth solicitor Edwin Dodshon. Through Church Knowle writer and campaigner Monica Hutchings I then obtained an old album of the Bond family from Tyneham House.

Many snapshots are delightfully homely but there are occasional professional gems by Walter Pouncy from Dorchester and Helen Muspratt at Swanage. Two of them were blown out of her studio window by a German bomb and picked up in the street.

This unique archive comes into its own in the Isle of Purbeck. It evokes another Dorset that was eliminated by the expansion of the Lulworth tank gunnery ranges, six days before Christmas in 1943, and even the hills that remained in civilian ownership are seen in another age. From horse-drawn reapers through to stone mining they did things differently there. Into the twentieth century, boulders were still being lowered from derricks at Dancing Ledge into offshore boats, as pleasure seekers climbed and bathed nearby. On St Alban's Head, men of the Coastguard service hauled their ropes from a shed to the cliffs, and fired them with rockets in a training exercise.

Uncle Frank, a house painter, had worked as a child for booksellers Horace G. Commin Limited in Old Christchurch Road, Bournemouth. Four decades later I was adopted by its current proprietor, the late John Ruston, and regularly treated to what he called 'a meal with Horace' as well as the nucleus of one of the best hoards of Dorset books and ephemera.

All the material here has come from my own collection. The theme is a combination of work and leisure that is punctuated by episodes of severe weather from bygone times. This selection of 350 shots concentrates without apology on the nostalgic. Mostly they are previously unpublished. Faces abound and many people will see themselves or their forebears. The list of subjects, in alphabetical order, tells the story. I'll intersperse the images with whatever whimsical snippets come to mind.

Bournemouth bookseller John Ruston, setting off from Poole on a circuit of the Purbeck coast, who encouraged Rodney Legg to collect his own Dorset archive.

ALMSHOUSES

St Margaret's Hospital and the chapel of St Margaret and St Anthony at Pamphill, on the outskirts of Wimborne, in 1895.

Henry Poulter, an inmate of the Hospital of St John the Baptist and St John the Evangelist, Sherborne, who died in the Almshouse on 7 August 1920.

Left: *Wimborne's old Chain Gate* (right), *in 1895, across the bottom of St Margaret's Hill beside St Margaret's Hospital* (centre) *at the junction with Cowgrove Road* (left).

The thirteenth-century chapel and a cluster of almshouses, on St Margaret's Hill, date from the sixteenth to eighteenth centuries, are on the site of a leper hospital that was established before 1241.

The picture joins young and old in conversation and this link between the generations was institutionalised at another almshouse in the parish. That on Pamphill Green is combined with the village school, under the same roof, in an imaginative piece of seventeenth-century architectural social engineering.

The common cause across the generations sums up the origins of the present book. As a child, collecting the material that has become this book half a century later, I soon came to realise why grandchildren empathise with their grandparents. They share a common enemy.

The ancient buildings, dating from 1437, survive intact and present-day residents show visitors around, as I found when I cycled to Sherborne from Bournemouth in 1962.

Almshouses are as English as cream teas, cricket on the village green, and Radio 4 on the wireless. I often think that we would fear old age less if, instead of contending with an evaporating pension fund, we could look forward to the certainty of a place in an historic almshouse. They offer dignity and respect, and a caring compromise between companionship and independence, under ancient foundation deeds laced with Biblical charity. To qualify for entry, feebleness, impotency and poverty were essential virtues. The settings are replete with flowers and shrubs, just yards away from the bustle of life and commerce that pass by on the other side of the garden gate.

ANCESTORS

Above: *Excavation of the Bronze Age round barrow in Shapwick Marsh, on the west bank of the River Stour in the parish of Sturminster Marshall, as depicted in* The Barrow Diggers, *by Charles Woolls, in 1839.*

Right: *Skull from a Bronze Age burial inserted into the south-west end of the Neolithic-period Wor Barrow on Handley Down, Sixpenny Handley, excavated by Lieutenant-General Augustus Pitt-Rivers in November 1893.*

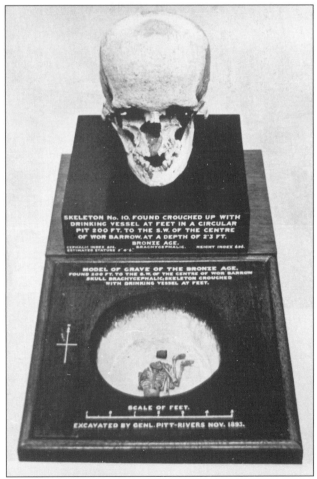

Left: *Iron Age skeletons in situ at Maiden Castle, excavated by Mortimer Wheeler, on 22 August 1937.*

Below: *One of the defenders of Maiden Castle, slaughtered by the Roman Second Legion Augusta which stormed the hill-fort after the Claudian invasion of AD 43, uncovered during Mortimer Wheeler's excavations in 1937.*

Left: *The excavations at the eastern end of Maiden Castle, looking northwards to Poundbury Farm and the avenue of trees* (top) *along the Bridport road into Dorchester, in 1937.*

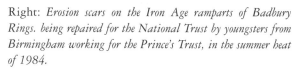

Right: *Erosion scars on the Iron Age ramparts of Badbury Rings. being repaired for the National Trust by youngsters from Birmingham working for the Prince's Trust, in the summer heat of 1984.*

Service in the freshly uncovered eastern end of the ruins of Shaftesbury Abbey, excavated by Edward Doran Webb, in 1904.

An obsession with our ancestors led me to cycle and hitch-hike across Dorset throughout the 1960s. My constant companion was a copy of the county's pages from the *List of Ancient Monuments in England*, complete with map references, duly ticked off as each batch of targets was reached.

Stone circles, burial mounds, hill-forts, castles and abbeys all figured in the expeditions. From Ronald Jessup I acquired a Celtic-style head in Portland stone which was found by his father, on a visit to Maiden Castle while stationed near Dorchester during the Second World War. It was protruding from a footpath scar in the ditches near the main entrance. With it came a letter from Sir Mortimer Wheeler, signed Rik, on British Academy notepaper dated 23 October 1957:

'Many thanks for sending me the curious stone head who arrived safely from the cavernous bowels of Ailsa's vile car. He is, as you rightly surmised, neither classical in workmanship or inspiration but rather belongs to the world of the Celts, and in particular, their barbarous fascination with the tete coupee. I was shown a number of similar examples while at Stanwix and I believe them to be widely distributed in the hinterland of the [Hadrian's] Wall.

As to his supposed provenance, we never saw anything comparable at Maiden Castle, but the circumstances of his acquisition seem to make an origin in that locality quite likely. The great monuments have a considerable place in local folklore.

He has rather a presence – not an antiquity for the faint-hearted!'

Sir Mortimer Wheeler captured the romance of the Wessex hill-forts in *Still Digging*, his autobiography, in 1955:

'It is, I think, fair to say that the excavation of Maiden Castle – of such small part of it as came within our compass – touched the imaginations of others than ourselves. T.E. Lawrence stood shyly watching us on the eve of his sudden death. Sir Arthur Evans,

small and frail, was blown across our skyline like an autumn leaf before the south-wester which was our normal accompaniment. Sir Frederic Kenyon, as President of the Society of Antiquaries, paid us regular courtesy calls – and, as an unrepentant boy, joined us in a Weymouth fun-fair afterwards. Augustus John and a picturesque entourage might, for a while, temper his science with our art. The poet Drinkwater, solemnly poised on the precarious edge of a pit, might offer his services as our laureate. But it is not of such that I speak when I recall the imaginative appeal of our enterprise.

I have in mind the hundreds of little folk from shops and factories and back-kitchens, who steamed on to the hill-top, day after day, and listened to our lecturettes which my students were carefully drilled to offer them, and put their pennies and their shillings into the box or maybe spoke their thanks. Years afterwards, in diverse parts of the world, I have come across all manner of people, from privates to peers, who had looked over our shoulders or grubbed upon their hands and knees on that hill-top.'

The indoor shrines to the county's prehistory, in order of significance, were the Pitt-Rivers Museum at Farnham, Dorset County Museum in Dorchester, and the Red House Museum at Christchurch. I was among the last to see the Pitt-Rivers collection intact, alone as a visitor with just the cleaner for company, shortly before the death of Captain George Pitt-Rivers in 1966. This was followed by haphazard dispersals, almost amounting to looting, during which a few items came in my direction. The bulk of the local material eventually found its way to Salisbury Museum.

The spell and spirit of Pitt-Rivers can still be felt across the chalklands of Cranborne Chase. His unique scheme for displaying ethnological anthropology survives in a second Pitt-Rivers Museum – in Oxford – where cluttered cases display a crazy cornucopia of objects that have been brought together as comparative examples of their subject matter rather than for either period or provenance.

ANTIQUITIES

Left: *Damaged Venus rising from the waves, surrounded by dolphins, from the apse of a Roman villa discovered at Hemsworth, near Witchampton, in 1831.*

Below: *Saxon angel, from the rood in the pre-Conquest nave at Winterbourne Steepleton, since reset in the north wall of St Michael's Church.*

The Pitt-Rivers Museum at Farnham, as it was from the 1880s till 1966, built as a Gypsy School in the 1850s.

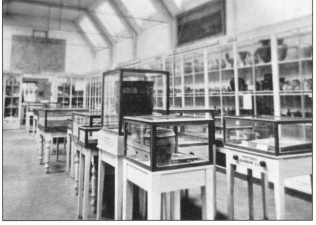

Bronze Age urns and other finds from Cranborne Chase in the former Pitt-Rivers Museum.

The prehistoric sarsens of Nine Stones, inside railings erected by the Ministry of Works, beside the A35 at Winterbourne Abbas.

Archaeological finds from Dorset were the spur to my search for field monuments. At a time when Roger Peers and Jocelyn Toynbee were excavating and describing the Roman floor featuring the head of Christ, which blacksmith William White had stumbled across in Hinton St Mary in September 1963, I was picking up tesserae cubes beside a ploughed public path at Hemsworth, between former Tarrant Rushton Aerodrome and Witchampton. The footpath has since been diverted but then passed the ruin of Walls Cottage which took its name from the Roman foundations beneath that grain field.

They had yielded a mosaic depicting dolphins on its surround, around a badly damaged Venus, in a tessellated floor that was lifted by Lord Alington of Crichel House and presented to the British Museum.

The much more elaborate Hinton St Mary floor, almost intact and with Chi-Rho iconography, was destined to become the centrepiece for new Romano-British displays in the British Museum. Then, tragically, it was dismantled to provide room for a different layout, and is now reduced to pieces in storage boxes. Only its roundel survives on show. Captain George Pitt-Rivers was convinced it shows the Emperor Constantine, who adopted the Chi-Rho symbol as his standard, rather than Jesus Christ.

Other relics can be found in their setting. My favourite Saxon carving is the stone angel in the church of St Michael the Archangel, commander of Heaven's army, at Winterbourne Steepleton. The buildings of the Pitt-Rivers Museum, no longer with their contents, survive between Thickthorn Cross and New Town at Farnham. The museum was founded by General Augustus Pitt-Rivers, the father of scientific archaeology, and held the county's principal anthropological and ethnological collections from the 1880s till 1966. Folk memory, however, stretches back even further and locally it is called the Gypsy School, for an initiative which closed in 1855.

Looking somewhat incongruous, the Nine Stones stand or lie beside the A35 trunk road west of Winterbourne Abbas. These sarsen boulders, from nearby downland, were erected for some unknown ceremonial or religious purpose in the Bronze Age. They are now in captivity, behind railings, which were erected by the old Ministry of Works.

There is a gap in the circle which may have held a tenth stone. A second stone circle used to stand on the roadside verge a mile to the west beside the single surviving Broad Stone which is now lying flat and virtually invisible. I found the evidence for this, including a sketch of the stones, in 1980 when I transcribed and published the seventeenth-century manuscript of John Aubrey's *Monumenta Britannica*, after it had lain in the Bodleian Library at Oxford for three centuries.

Another lost circle was at Rempstone Gate between East Lulworth and Whiteway on the parish boundary where the former public road through Povington – itself now a lost hamlet in the middle of the Lulworth Ranges – crossed the parish boundary between East Lulworth and Tyneham. The stones were removed by a farmer named Bower for gateposts and a bridge over a stream.

That site was recorded by Victorian antiquary Charles Warne who also tells of what appears to have been a second Neolithic burial chamber only a quarter of a mile from the Hell Stone cromlech above Portesham. They stood immediately north-west of Black Down Barn, with anthropomorphic names – Jeffrey, Joan, Denty and Eddy.

Charles Warne recalled the site in 1864, though I doubt whether all four stones were the same size and equally spaced or it would make a nonsense of the rhyme:

'In a small valley, on the down of Portesham Farm, there stood within these last ten years, four upright stones – each about ten feet high – in a line and nearly equidistant from each other, to which was attached the following doggerel: "Jeffery and Joan, and their little dog Denty, with Eddy alone."

By the direction of the then occupier of the farm, Mr Maufield, these stones were removed and built in an adjoining wall. The neighbourhood abounding in stone, one would have thought he could have spared these interesting remains, but what is safe against ignorance and avarice combined.'

BATHCHAIRS

By the time I was born in Bournemouth, in 1947, the invalid carriage had seen its day. The only bathchair I ever saw was that placed in the entrance to the Russell Cotes Art Gallery and Museum in former East Cliff Hall. Bathchairs were named for fashionable Bath and soon spread to the southern spas of the English riviera, from Torquay to Southsea. Severely wounded in the South African War, Algy Bond of Tyneham House – the squire's eldest son – took to one for his return to the seaside, recuperating in the autumn of 1900.

When I first saw it, Bournemouth's specimen bathchair was in a twilight zone between use and display, parked as you would expect to find a wheelchair provided for disabled shoppers in the foyer of a modern supermarket.

Bournemouth claimed a climate that was beneficial to those suffering chronic illness and boasted an Invalids' Walk where such carriages were promenaded through the conifers and rhododendrons between Westover Road and the Lower Gardens. It was renamed Pine Walk when town councillors began to flinch at mention of such associations.

Rupert Brooke would have approved. 'Here Rupert Brooke 1887–1915 Discovered Poetry' the blue plaque reads at Grantchester Dean in Littledown Road, as I remember it, though the house is now attached to Dean Park Road, since the town's inner relief road swept away its neighbours. It was the home of his grandfather, Revd Richard England Brooke, and Rupert holidayed here. He found inspiration at West Lulworth, describing it as the most beautiful village in England, but despaired of Bournemouth's 'moaning pines' and was dismissive of its clientele: 'With decrepit and grey-haired invalids I drift wanly along the cliffs.'

The principal local supplier of 'spinal carriages, coaches, wheeled chairs and all kind of invalid furniture' was G.E. Bridge & Co. Ltd at 128 Christchurch Road, Bournemouth. The firm also advertised 'bandages, belts, trusses, deformity and orthopaedic appliances of every description' and by 1914 provided a 'transport service by motor ambulance'.

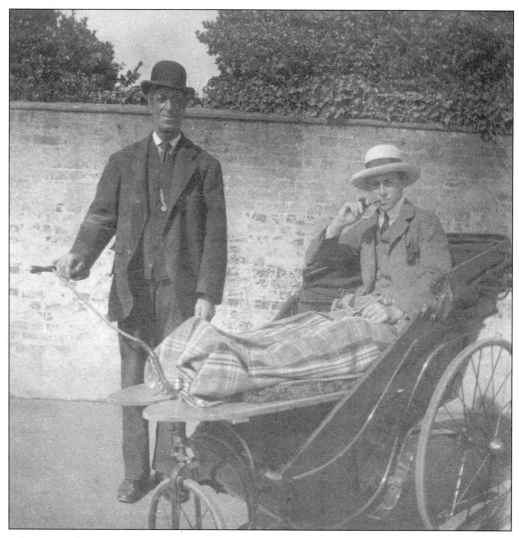

Algernon Bond and coachman Frederick Knight, from Tyneham, at Weymouth in September 1900.

BATHING

George III's bathing machine, on Weymouth sands, in 1909 which was the year when John A. Glover-Kinde wrote his famous song: 'I do like to be beside the seaside.'

Strip and swim was the morning ritual for the boys of Durnford School, Langton Matravers – watched by headmaster Thomas Pellatt – into the sea from Dancing Ledge in 1898.

Learning to swim, in the pool cut by quarrymen at Dancing Ledge, in 1908.

Diving from the swimming raft moored in Worbarrow Bay, by members of the Bond family in 1906.

Margaret Bond (left) making a splash, and 'Dan' in brother Ralph Bond's canoe, in Worbarrow Bay.

Above: *Studland Jetty in 1938 with five-year-old Christopher Horn and four-year-old Michael Walker, by Helen Muspratt.*

Above right: *Bathing at Swanage in the 1930s, also photographed by Helen Muspratt.*

Sea bathing was popularised in Dorset when King George III adopted Weymouth as 'the English Naples'. The holiday coast was born as we know it today though swimming was for the gentry and the children of Coastguards rather than cottagers and fishermen. The latter were adamant that the sea was a hostile element and that safety was better served by staying with one's boat. If it was doomed, that was your fate, and it was more humane to drown than struggle for survival.

'They should have stayed with their ship,' an old lady told Langton Matravers author Nina Warner Hooke when she researched the tragic loss of the steamship *Treveal* which split in half at the end of her maiden voyage, from Ceylon, in 1923. Both halves remained afloat, off Chapman's Pool, as if to taunt the crew who had abandoned ship. 'There's no back door to the sea,' was received wisdom in Purbeck fishing communities.

Two pictures from Studland and Swanage have had an eventful history. These were framed and displayed in the window of Miss Helen Muspratt's photographic studio at No. 10 Institute Road on Swanage seafront. They were picked up damaged in the street after the building was destroyed by a German bomb in April 1942.

Studland Jetty was already a memory as it had been demolished during the construction of anti-invasion defences in 1940. Its two young users from before the Second World War have been identified as Nottingham businessman Christopher Horn and Wing Commander Michael Walker, of the Royal Air Force, who was retired and back in Swanage by the end of the millennium.

BEACHES

'The Heroic Defender of Ladysmith and Charger' moulded by a 'self taught' ex-shunter from Clapham Junction, on Weymouth sands in 1903.

'Novelty in Sand' on Bournemouth beach, signed by S. Ponge between the 'British Lion on Guard' and 'A Wounded Friend' in 1910.

Soldier and Baby Jumbo collecting for the Daily Mirror *Christmas pudding appeal, on Bournemouth beach, in 1912.*

'The Great Sacrifice' commemorated by Weymouth sand artist Swift Vincent in 1921: 'Greater love hath no man than this – to lay down his life for his friend.'

Jesus Christ, prophetically wearing a cross at the Last Supper, as depicted on Weymouth beach in the 1960s.

Weymouth Esplanade and sands, northwards from the donkeys (centre foreground) *and Royal Hotel* (left) *to St John's Church and Brunswick Terrace* (centre right) *in 1910.*

Weymouth sands in the 1930s.

Dorset has some of the best beaches in Europe. South-facing sweeps of sand, such as the 7 miles from Sandbanks to Southbourne, are protected by cliffs from northerly winds. Even the east-facing beaches of Weymouth and Studland are shielded by the landscape from prevailing south-westerlies.

Beaches are generally for play but at the other extreme we were often treated to fine art. Sand artists produced amazing three-dimensional forms that were all the more wonderful for being fragile and transient. As with our sand castles, destined to be destroyed by the incoming tide, they were doomed from the moment of their making. Unlike the much less worthy creators of present-day installations for Tate Modern by Turner Prize Winners the sand artists received only pennies.

Greenhill and Weymouth Pier in the 1950s.

Channel Islands steamer, outward bound from Weymouth, with HMS Illustrious *in the background in 1948.*

BELLS

The eight historic bells of Wimborne Minster, grounded in 1911 when they were recast and rehung, with two new ones being added.

Resonating from that line by John Donne, about not asking for whom the bell tolls, the sound of bells punctuate memories of the twentieth century. There were school bells and church bells; ship bells and bicycle bells; division bells and Big Ben; wedding bells and funeral bells; warning bells and victory bells. For a whole generation the most welcome sound was silence – the absence of bells – through the first years of the Second World War as they would have signified German invasion.

All this is embraced by *Summoned by Bells*, published in 1960, which was the verse autobiography of Sir John Betjeman. The bells that proclaimed the turning point of the war with the Battle of Alamein, and again with Victory in Europe, have their American equivalent with a single bell in Independence Hall. The Liberty Bell was the first to be tolled after the passing of the Declaration of Independence.

'The bell is not the less sacred for now being cracked,' we are told. In fact it is appropriate, in that time can also toll for bells, and nothing can last for ever.

Mrs Winifred Legg's handbell team at Puddletown Primary School in 1949.

BOATING

Before the advent of the shipping forecast, lakes and estuaries were the only safe areas for boating in Dorset, which has an exposed coastline and a lack of canals. Although one was authorised by Parliament, in 1796, to link the Somerset collieries with the River Stour beside a turnpike road near Shillingstone, the project failed in the early nineteenth century. None of our rivers became navigable though there is a tradition for following the example of Jerome Klapka Jerome from Blandford and Wimborne to Christchurch. The Walsall-born humorist published *Three Men in a Boat* in 1889.

Right: Newly created lake in 50 acres of parkland at Moigne Combe, between Owermoigne and Crossways, where Henry Pomeroy Bond built 'a mansion of brick' in 1900.

Yachts in Poole Harbour, off Brownsea Island, in 1908.

BREWING

The Fookes Brothers' Milton Brewery in 1880, in thatched buildings at the south end of Milton Abbas which continued to produce beer until 1953.

Peter Gibbs, chairman of Gibbs Mew, arriving with shire-horses Danny and Dylan in a brewer's dray at the Star and Garter, Crescent Street, Weymouth, in about 1980.

In 1889, *Kelly's Directory* listed 32 brewers, producing beer in towns and villages across Dorset. Casks of ale and stout had a limited sell-by date and their distribution was limited by the range of the drayman. On the other hand, the Norwegian Block Ice Company was not only importing its principal product from across the North Sea but ensured it was 'sent securely packed in sacking and sawdust' from Portsea or Southampton – by boat, rail or carrier – to 'any town in Hampshire, Wiltshire, Dorsetshire and Sussex'. Speciality beers also travelled widely, in stoneware bottles, including Styring's Tisbury stout and Coombe and Co's London stout.

This could be a two-way traffic. James Panton rebuilt former Gillingham's Malthouse at Swanage which had been gutted by fire on 8 November 1854. He revived a product which had been made in the town since the Napoleonic Wars though production ceased soon after the railway arrived beside Swanage Brewery which was demolished in 1893. Meanwhile, *Kelly's Directory* enthused:

'The properties of the water are considered as good as those of Burton-on-Trent, as analysed by Doctors Letherby and Graham, and is exclusively used by Messrs. Panton at their brewery, the produce of which has long been characteristically known as "Swanage Pale Ale".'

BRIDGES

Colber Bridge over the Stour at Sturminster Newton, overlooked by the Hive (top left) *and Riverside Villas* (top right) *where Thomas Hardy wrote* The Return of the Native, *photographed by Sydney S. Carruthers in 1892.*

Darkhole Bridge in Melbury Park, with guests of the Fox-Strangways family from Melbury House, in 1912.

Georgian transportation threat on Town Bridge at Sturminster Newton, on a cast-iron notice dating from 1820, photographed with the antithesis of a vandal a century later.

Above: *The narrow Norman stone arches of South Bridge across the River Frome at Wareham – seen from the tower of Lady St Mary parish church – shortly before demolition for a concrete replacement in 1926.*

Right: *Five Bridges at Lower Nyland, near Kington Magna, before demolition in the 1960s for diverting and widening the A30.*

Below: *Swanny river and mediaeval Horton Bridge, across the River Allen, in the foothills of Cranborne Chase.*

It is easy to become passionate about bridges. They are the characterful crossing points that mark one's progress across the landscape. Many in Dorset are scheduled ancient monuments, dating back to Plantagenet times (though Wareham's was even earlier), usually on sites where the predecessor was a ford. Dorset would also have had its Roman bridges.

Mediaeval structures make use of local stone, ranging from brown heathstone in the east and the familiar grey of Purbeck rock, through to golden browns in the Hamstone belt towards Somerset. Huge cutwaters defy flash-floods, splitting the threatening force of turbulent waters, but it takes more than the visible structure to attach a thousand tons of masonry to the riverbed. Below there will be oak piles, waterlogged but saved from decay by permanently anaerobic conditions.

Humped bridges belong to the past. These days flat slabs of steel and concrete support dual carriageways with hardly any indication when seen from the highway. There is just one steel suspension bridge in Dorset, but that only carries a footpath, across the Stour on the upstream side of Canford School.

BUSES

Bere Regis bus and driver in the late 1940s.

Bere Regis and District Motor Services (telephone number Bere Regis 56) dated from before the Second World War. Their familiar buses, rustic in appearance with a dingy chocolate-brown livery, were owned by Reginald William Toop, from North Street. He had parted from rival omnibus owner George Vacher in 1929. Vacher then sold out to Hants and Dorset Motor Services, in 1930, but remained running their local office beside No. 31 West Street until retirement in the 1950s.

To a post-war suburban boy, from Bournemouth, the world revolved around the Square and its Omnibus and Coach Station beside Exeter Road. Built in bunker-like concrete, of the austere functional architecture which Norman Mailer dubbed as 'airport modern', this temple to transport was shared by the common green buses of Hants & Dorset Motor Services and the regal-liveried coaches of Royal Blue Automobile Services.

Greyhound coaches took us on day trips, hopefully to capital destinations, though more often an outing to somewhere just beyond walking distance, such as the New Forest. Shamrock & Rambler cornered much of the granny market but had their own depot, beyond the Lansdowne, in Holdenhurst Road. That promised an excursion into premature ageing.

Bournemouth Coach Station in 1954.

Greyhound coach from Bournemouth with visitors to Rufus Stone, in the New Forest, in 1955.

'Taylor and Co, Purveyors' the sign reads, above the Wimborne butcher's rows of prize heifers and steers, in a Christmas display in the High Street from about 1903.

Transatlantic and Empire food began filling the shops in late Victorian times. Cheap land overseas, plus railroads to the seaboard and bulk storage in steamers, conspired to ensure that much of Britain's meat was imported by the turn of the twentieth century. Prices dipped as carriage costs dropped. Whereas it cost 2.5d per pound to ship mutton from New Zealand to Britain in 1882, this had been slashed to a halfpenny a pound by 1898. During this period total meat imports increased from 5 to 18 million hundredweight a year.

David Jones (left) *explaining cutting techniques to a trainee at Case and Sons Limited's bacon plant in Motcombe in the 1970s.*

CARAVANS

Haystack (left) *in a field sharing a 'Tents for Hire' sign and one of the first caravans* (right) *in the Jordan valley between Preston and Bowleaze Cove, with a battleship moored in Weymouth Bay* (top left) *in 1935.*

On 17 June 2005 I was invited to put the case on Radio Solent that caravans are a blot on the landscape. My counterpart spoke for the Caravan Club but I opened the debate as a veteran environmental campaigner – since the 1960s – against coastal caravan camps in Dorset. These overlooked Durdle Door, when seen from the sea, and still cover an entire valley east of Weymouth, as well as sites at Charmouth, Eype, West Bay, Burton Bradstock and Fleet.

My suggestion from 1970 that such establishments should be scooped up and placed in Moreton gravel pits has partly come to pass. Dorset's answer to Center Parcs are now sited there and perfectly screened behind dense vegetation. Even the most unsightly of the seaside camps have had beneficial side-effects, having stimulated the Enterprise Neptune initiative of the National Trust. This captured the public imagination, raising funds that have saved many miles of what is now a World Heritage Site, in order to prevent such camps from spreading and sprawling into each other.

Seaview Camp (foreground) *and Bowleaze Cove* (top left), *filling the Jordan valley with caravans during the post-war return to the seaside, in 1951.*

Seaview Camp densely-packed with vans of all shapes and sizes in 1959.

FXX 476 (centre left) and hundreds similar at Waterside Camp, Preston, in 1955.

CARS

The first car to have a Lyme Regis owner was this De Dion Bouton, with R. Wallace giving a ride to Spike Hardy, in 1902.

Lord and Lady Alington stand beside the 24-horsepower Leon Bollee FX 2 (right), hosting Dorset Automobile Club's rally at Crichel House in May 1906.

Chauffeur stops in the fields of Barton Home Farm, south-west of Cerne Abbas, in 1910.

Car and 'Garage' sign, on the wall of the Fleur-de-Lis (centre) at Cranborne, photographed by Bournemouth solicitor Edwin Dodshon on 17 June 1916.

Above: *Sir Alec Coryton and his De Dion Bouton, both in active retirement at Langton Matravers, in the 1970s.*

Left: *Bournemouth-registered car stopped at Kettle Tea Room, next to Picket Post Hotel, where the A31 enters the New Forest above Ringwood, in 1950.*

The motorised 1950s, with cars and buses on both sides of the High Street at Shaftesbury between Joseph Frisby Ltd's shoe shop (left) *and the Town Hall.*

As long ago as 1904, writing in the *Bournemouth Graphic*, G.E. Bridge could look back on the 1890s as 'the early days of the motor car' and refer to events 'that could not happen now' on his first car journey. He omitted to give the year, or the name of his male companion, or even the maker of the 'good car' which might have been 'a Panhard, Dijon, Napier, or what, and I do not think the real maker would care to recognise it'.

She (the gender of his vehicle throughout his account) and his friend's chauffeur took them from the Grand Hotel, Bournemouth, to Sherborne School, in order to visit their respective offspring at half term. The outward journey, which began at 9.00 am after 'a short delay in the arrival of the necessary petrol', turned into 'a splendid run' through Wimborne and Blandford. They reached the Digby Hotel, Sherborne, in three hours. Lunch and 'schoolboy tea-making in their studies' were followed by an afternoon departure and thoughts of 'arriving home for a late dinner'.

In two miles they ground to a halt with a puncture. Changing the tyre took 55 minutes, but the replacement turned out to be defective, though the next change was accomplished in just 40 minutes. They came to a stop again while 'in climbing gear' as the vehicle struggled up the slope above Enford Farm between Shillingstone and Durweston. It was 6.45 pm, 'dark, and very chilly' and despite the 'putting in and out of innumerable plugs, examining coils, testing cells, and turning the wretched handle in front, she refused absolutely to respond to our attention'.

Mr Bridge was given a lift to Blandford by a gentleman in a dog-cart, and treated to supper in a hotel, having resigned himself to catching the train. Then came 'the unmistakable thud of my friend's car' and a cheery shout: 'She's all right, my boy. It was nothing but the sparker.'

It was 9.30 pm, and they were on the road again, but 'everything seemed to go wrong, and to make matters worse we got off the track,' finding themselves stuck in a hollow beside a farmhouse and forced to wake the inhabitants for help and directions. Having crossed the country 'through a certain gate' they found themselves on the Cranborne road

between Horton Inn and Wimborne. The next halt – 'cause obscure' – was in sight and sound of the chimes of Wimborne Minster. They pushed the motor car away from houses before 'turning that dreadful handle' in 'fruitless efforts which threatened dislocation of the shoulder'.

Eventually the pair abandoned the vehicle, with the chauffeur, and woke a hostler at an inn who harnessed a horse to drive them to Bournemouth. The car owner was dropped off at his home and Mr Bridge was delivered to the Grand Hotel, at 4 am, 'muffled to the eyebrows in furs and oilskins'. The night porter initially refused to provide the Wimborne coachman with refreshment. He relented as the traveller shed his wraps and suspicion turned to recognition: 'Gracious me, it's Mr Bridge. What would the coachman like, sir?'

One of the last living links with those experiences and contemporary vehicles was Air Chief Marshal Sir Alec Coryton (1895–1981), who retired as chief executive of guided weapons at the Ministry of Supply in 1951.

He lived at Two Leas, Langton Matravers, where I came across him during my explorations of the Isle of Purbeck. He told me that his 'pride and joy, as a labour of love,' was the restoration of a 1902 De Dion Bouton. It had been bought in Italy in 1910 by Daniel Hanbury from Castle Malwood, Lyndhurst. Hanbury's daughter, Philippa, married Alec Coryton who found the derelict motor car locked in a shed in the New Forest.

The registration letters FX and PR for Dorset and EL, LJ and RU for Bournemouth remain current but there is a story behind their introduction a century ago. Dorset was initially issued with BF as its first prefix but the Lord Lieutenant fired off the following salvo in a letter to Whitehall:

'If you pause for a moment to reflect what the military man in the street is going to think of my passing, then you will realise my hesitation at accepting the designation Bloody Fool One.'

As a result FX was substituted, and BF issued to Staffordshire, apparently without complaint.

CARTS

The Cart Shed at Studland, across the road from Manor Farm
– seen in about 1905 – still has a thatched roof and a cart a
century later.

John Hatchard's wagon from Walford Mill, Wimborne, in 1908.

Kelp collecting at Seatown, from beneath Golden Cap, in 1913.

Above: *The Market Square at Sturminster Newton, cluttered with carts on a Monday – its market day – in the 1920s, looking northwards to the Police Station* (centre).

Below: *Coming into Rodwell Avenue from Kempston Road, Weymouth, in 1933.*

Cart-ride at Milton Abbas during the village bi-centenary celebrations of 1973.

Horse-drawn carts were the mainstay of land transport for three millennia. Each town and village had its carriers, and every business its wagons, until the universal spread of motor transport after the First World War. Carriers trundle through the novels of Thomas Hardy under their dialect name of tranters. John Betjeman chose to conclude his poem 'Dorset' with the lines 'While Tranter Reuben, Gordon Selfridge, Edna Best and Thomas Hardy lie in Mellstock Churchyard now.'

CHAPEL

Left: *Dennis Bailey in the Congregational Chapel at Cripplestyle, Alderholt, which his ancestor William Bailey created, still standing but derelict and doomed in 1969.*

Crumbling cob and failing thatch behind the brick frontage of Cripplestyle Chapel in 1972.

Many parish churches became redundant in the late twentieth century but there was a far greater attrition rate among non-conformist places of worship. Most were converted into houses but some, inevitably, suffered a complete demise.

The thatched-roofed chapel at Cripplestyle was opened on 11 December 1807:

'Though but a very plain, humble structure, it was dear to the people, as one which their own willing hands had helped to raise.'

King Barrow, the nearby heathland knoll, is a gorse-covered natural hillock rather than an ancient burial mound as its name might suggest. It rises above the hamlet of Cripplestyle in the north-east corner of the county. Traditionally there has been a pilgrimage to its summit on Whit Thursday. That day in 1807, 'the chief cottage preacher' of the locality, William Bailey is said to have led his flock up the hill from the partly-built Ebenezer Chapel at Cripplestyle and hoisted a banner:

'Feed my Lambs.' Groups from other Congregational and non-conformist fellowships in the area used to attend the annual event as a tribute to the 'Cripplestyle pioneers' who had built the mud-walled chapel. In 1861, when a new schoolroom was built, a thousand people followed a brass band to the summit.

An alternative conventionally-built chapel was then provided in Alderholt village, in 1888, and named the Williams Memorial Chapel as a tribute to Samuel Williams who looked after the Cripplestyle building for many decades. His eleven sons and daughters raised £100 towards the £700 cost of the Alderholt replacement for the 'unsightly and unsuitable' Cripplestyle Chapel.

To others, however, it was picturesque. Devotees kept it going for another half a century but then came years of neglect. Cripplestyle Chapel eventually collapsed, in the 1970s, but its site is now a memorial garden. Several acres of heathland at King Barrow also remain accessible, as open country, having been registered as common land.

CIDER

Basket of apples (right foreground) *and a full hopper* (right background) *ready for cider-making beside E. Hatcher's screw-press, at Hinton St Mary, in the 1890s.*

Cider applies tended to be small and hard. Look at large-scale Ordnance Survey maps for the Somerset-Dorset borderlands at the turn of the century, for parishes like Charlton Horethorne and Buckhorn Weston, and you will see that most of the fields in the centre of the villages are devoted to orchards.

One of the favourite Dorset-grown trees was the medium bitter-sweet Yarlington Mill variety which took its name from a farm between Yarlington and Galhampton in south Somerset. It was a mid-season apple, picked in the first three weeks of November, and noted for high yields. Usually it was mixed with smaller quantities of other varieties, to improve the quality, as it otherwise produced what was described as 'light rather than vintage' liquor.

COASTGUARD

Officers, men and auxiliaries of His Majesty's Coast Guard Station No. 300, on St Alban's Head at Worth Matravers, in the 1920s.

Rocket life-saving apparatus, stored in two Board of Trade wagons, being removed from the Coast Guard depot, beside Coastguard Cottages on St Alban's Head, in the 1920s.

Preparing the mortar to fire a maroon shell on St Alban's Head, to a backdrop of its Coastguard Cottages and Norman chapel (top right).

Firing the line in the Coast Guard exercise, at St Alban's Head, from the clifftop above disused quarries on the 350-feet promontory.

Using a breeches-buoy around an obviously able-bodied 'casualty' who is being winched to safety, at St Alban's Head, to complete the Coast Guard training exercise.

His Majesty's Coast Guard – these were separate words until the relatively recent reform of Her Majesty's Coastguard – not only policed the nation's shore for the Customs and Excise service but produced eyes on the ground for calling out the Lifeboat. Since 1856, under Admiralty governance, it has provided the nationwide command and control facilities for tackling maritime emergencies.

The great advance in the ability of the Coast Guard to intervene in rescues from the shore came through rocketry in 1878. Major-General Edward Boxer, superintendent of the Royal Laboratory at Woolwich Arsenal devised a life-saving rope-carrying rocket apparatus. Fired from land, to vessels stranded offshore, it saved hundreds of lives.

Each of our Coast Guard Stations had its rocket shed. The technology was further refined by the Shermuly Company of Dartford, makers of distress flares, in the process of which Boxet's two-stage missile was replaced by a simple single-stage motor. Rocket apparatus remains in service use, though these days most of the dramatic rescues are at the end of a vertical line, dangling from a helicopter.

COBBLERS

Puddletown shoe-maker Robert Rowland in 1891.

Langton Matravers shoe-mender Thomas Saunders at Acton in 1905.

As a cobbler's son I can attest to the adage about having the worst shoes, though as much as anything that was due to the physical requirements of long, pointed feet which were ill-suited to traditional leather footwear. I showed no aptitude for the trade and the only fact associated with it which I remember is that St Crispin is the patron saint of shoemakers. He is much better known, in the national psyche, for his place in Shakespeare's *Henry V* inspiring the 'band of brothers' who would shed their blood 'upon Saint Crispin's day'. The Battle of Agincourt took place on 25 October 1415.

Retired bootmaker Henry Critchell, with his wife, outside No. 5 Grove Lane, Abbotsbury, in 1923.

Ted Legg, the author's father (right) at his last, in the 1950s, on Peters Hill, Winton, Bournemouth.

COMMONS

Cottage and common, with its pond, in the Frome valley near Dorchester, photographed by Walter Pouncy in the 1890s.

Despite centuries of enclosures, relict areas of common land survive across Dorset, with those that were registered as such now having a right of public access for air and exercise. They came about, however, as a means of providing shared grazing lands to cottagers and other rights that could be held in common included peat-digging and collecting dead-wood and gorse-sticks for fuel.

Moral therapeutic values were seen in country walking by the seventeenth-century parson and poet George Herbert, of Bemerton, Wiltshire, who regarded rogationtide ceremonies in which the Church continued pagan practices of the beating the bounds, as more than a means of ensuring the integrity and preservation of boundaries. Leading his flock around the edge of the parish was also an exercise in practical spirituality, thought the rector who set them the example of a saint: 'Charity, in loving walking and neighbourly accompanying one with another, with reconciling of differences at that time, if they be any.'

The pound at Langton Herring, where stray stock was impounded, with Dorset publisher Peter Shaw giving scale to the graveyard wall at the rear, in 1990.

New Street, Puddletown, in the summer of 1910.

Residents young and old of the cottages at Gold Hill below the perimeter wall of mediaeval Shaftesbury Abbey, in 1900.

Church Lane, formerly Parson's Lane, and children from the Elementary School in Owermoigne, in 1908.

Right: *Chalking the pavement for hop-scotch, at Corfe Castle, in 1907.*

Below: *Edwardian glimpse up Red Lane, at Abbotsbury, with the elderly cottager having gathered his burden from Knolls withy beds, half a mile away above Ferny Hole.*

Pond Cottage at Up Cerne with Edwardian occupants.

Two ladies, each with a cat in their arms, at The Folly, Cerne Abbas, in 1907.

Retired sheep-breeder Wilfred Cake and his eighteenth-century home at Sherford Farm, near Morden Park Corner, in 1972.

When I met 72-year-old Wilfred Cake and his wife, Ivy, they were living as tenants in an eighteenth-century farmhouse near Morden Park Corner. The thatch had collapsed through their bedroom ceiling and elder, ash, holly and grass grew from the roof above. Polythene was everywhere to catch the water as it streamed down. Ivy sacrificed the side-piece from her mahogany table to bolster the bulging ceiling.

'It's fairly dry inside – except when it rains,' Wilfred remarked wryly. He fought at Ypres and the Somme and was then taken prisoner by the Germans after shrapnel smashed his ankle in the trenches of the Hindenburg Line. The Great War over, he came back to farming and was a champion Dorset-horn sheep breeder, at Lower Burton, near Dorchester, until he was put out of business by foot and mouth restrictions in the pandemic of the 1930s. Rams he had already sold to Australians at 100 guineas a time were impounded on his farm and finally realised £3 as butchers' meat.

The Cakes knew the hard life for most of the twentieth century. When I interviewed them, in the autumn of 1972, their names had been on the application list for a council house at Westport House, the offices of what was then Wareham and Purbeck Rural District Council, for the past ten years. Councillors had come and gone but this elderly couple remained as silent names through a succession of housing committees.

Sherford Farm, a property of the Morden Estates, controlled by Drax family from Charborough Park, had been given a bathroom with the help of a government grant. At the time, 1161 acres that had been owned by Admiral Sir Reginald Aylmer Ranfurley Plunkett-Ernle-Erle-Drax – who died aged 87 in 1968 – had recently passed to Lieutenant-Commander Walter Drax. A further 11,889 acres were managed by the Morden Estates Company. Sherford Farm became a test case with press and television coverage.

Though retired, Wilfred Cake was keeping a mile of river clear of weeds, upstream for a mile, from the farm to lakes in Morden Park. Martin Fortescue, the land agent from Charborough, had visited the Cakes two years earlier and told them that the farmhouse was no longer worth repairing.

The situation then, as explained by Wilfred Cake, reflected law and practice across feudal Dorset as it had been practised for generations:

'They won't do anything. They told me they won't repair it and I have to get out. We have got no where else to go. They did a bit of thatch once, about seven years ago, and my son paid for it, I think. I work for them when they ask and I don't get anything for it, but I live in the house. I've got the cottage and I don't pay rent. So I do odd jobs for nothing. They can't get us out before they get us accommodation but they will win because the cottage lets the water in.'

Cottage clearances around Morden reached a peak in the 1960s. Dozens of cob and thatch buildings were razed to the ground, particularly in and around the twin villages of East Morden and West Morden, and in the hamlet at Cockett Hill. There were 'the scars of 34 demolished or decaying buildings', it was reported in 1967, and since then the cottage of Mr and Mrs Alfred Creech had been demolished opposite West Morden Farm, and that facing Ernle Farm was demolished in 1968. The small but attractive No. 35 West Morden, tenanted by Mrs Elsie Crocker, was also pulled down that summer.

At Whitefield, beside a stream that runs down to Morden Park and Lytchett Bay, a cosy mud-walled thatched cottage was standing empty in the shadow of a huge pear tree on the day when I called at the stables in Charborough Park to hear Martin Fortescue's side of the story, on 25 September 1972.

Marked on the map, at Whitefield, there were a range of three cottages, a mill, and a cottage opposite. These had disappeared. All that survived of the southern part of Whitefield hamlet was this one cottage with the pear tree, beside the clear stream that was the haunt of the kingfisher and otter, with No. 53 on the door. This was its number in the Morden rent roll. Most of the other numbers that were once neighbours were now extinct.

Mrs Jennifer Simpson, who owned the village stores in Winterborne Kingston, told me the story of No. 53. Its last occupant had been Mrs Ethel Belcher. Despite the cramped conditions, she ran a pre-school nursery. Mrs Simpson feared that No. 53 would now go the way of its former neighbours:

Fiery finale for Sherford Farm, on 22 January 1973, after which the site was cleared and flattened.

'Today it is difficult to see where these other cottages stood. Their gardens are tangled with brushwood, nettles and brambles and the land is clearly of no benefit to anyone. In the village of Morden the same estate has been gradually eliminating similar cottages in much greater numbers. Is there no way of protecting these few remaining Dorset cottages from the ruthless bulldozer and equally ruthless landowner.'

I put these points to Mr Fortescue and asked if they would consider selling No. 53, as it stood on the edge of the estate, rather than at its heart, and might have raised £10,000 at that time. It was doomed, however, as the following day the water was cut off. When I arrived with a photographer on 10 October 1972 it had been bulldozed into a heap. Poignantly, we found Mrs Belcher's easel, propped against the pear tree.

Commander Drax defended the estate's policy over its surplus buildings, after saying that people mattered most:

'What we are trying to do is preserve the best. Each cottage obviously has got to be decided on its merits and these are some of the factors which we take into account – its condition; its site; and then its siting. This, say, may be on a dangerous corner. I'm thinking of Vine Cottage at Morden, a nice one which I would like to keep anywhere else, but it was on a corner and made it dangerous. A site in the village has to be considered in its relationship to the church, post office, public house and the community as a whole. Then there is the cost of putting it in good order.'

He declined the opportunity for further comment on what he dismissed as one-sided gutter journalism. Ironically it was my magazine article, on the plight of Ivy and Wilfred Cake and their ten-year wait on the housing list, that prompted officials into action. Mr and Mrs Cake were rehoused in a council property at East Morden. Sherford Farm, stuffed with straw bales, was burnt down by two estate workers on 22 January 1973.

Another sequel was that having urged the creation of a green belt around the Bournemouth conurbation, I gave the estate the credit for successfully holding back Poole and its suburbs, where the planners had failed:

'The building line of the Poole satellite estates of Corfe Mullen, Lytchett Matravers, Upton and Lytchett Minster collapses when it meets the Berlin Wall of the Drax hedgerows. Ruthless conservation, Drax style, has preserved a gigantic block of some of the most fragile, yet speculatively valuable landscape in Dorset.'

It was a point which I reiterated in June 2005. The green belt needed all the help it could get and provided my theme as guest speaker at the summer fete of Dorset branch of the Campaign for the Protection of Rural England in the grounds of Bingham's Melcombe House. Many of the cottages have gone but the Morden Estate remains as green as ever.

No. 53 Whitefield, typical of those on the Morden Estate that were redundant and uninhabited, in the summer of 1972.

The end of No. 53 Whitefield, reduced to slabs of mud-walling and heaps of thatch, in October 1972.

CRICKET

Village cricketer George Whieldon of Wyke House, Gillingham, painted in 1845.

The portrait of George Whieldon, wearing a top-hat, dates from the year in which cricket progressed from a country pastime into a national institution. In 1845 the 'gentleman's game' went on a 'cricket crusade' as the All England XI travelled the country. This saw the start of the scoreboards, practice nets and mowing machines. It remained, however, a pursuit of the upper classes and was the subject of much gambling. Lord Frederick Beauclerk, a famous amateur cricketer, wagered as much as 1000 guineas on a game and claimed to make annual profits in excess of £6000.

Because of the association with betting and gambling, cricket was frowned upon in polite society, and many gentleman players adopted pseudonyms.

Nicholas Wanostrocht moved from Brighton to Wimborne, to No. 1 Julians Villas (now 23 Julians Road), in 1872. He died there and is buried in the town's cemetery under a stone which tells us no more than his dates. Nicholas Wanostrocht was born on 5 October 1804 and died on 3 September 1876. To his friends and contemporaries he was Nicholas Felix, the author in 1845 of the cricketing classic *Felix on the Bat*, the frontispiece of which shows him wielding a bat as he flies above the field on the back of a huge mammalian bat.

Former Wimborne bookseller William Hoade, who rediscovered Felix's association with the town, showed me a rare undamaged copy of the book and explained that it was often in poor condition because copies were taken into the field as an instruction manual.

Nicholas Wanostrocht's teacher had been Harry Hampton of East Surrey Cricket Club. As Nicholas Felix, the left-handed player made his first recorded appearance at Thomas Lord's cricket ground in 1828, and famously paired with Alfred Mynn of Kent Cricket Club, in 1834.

Wanostrocht designed a 'Catapulta' automatic ball-throwing machine for professional-speed bowling in the practice nets. He also invented ribbed batting gloves and introduced various protective 'paddings' to guard against the 'uncertainty and irregularity' inherent in throwing styles.

T.M. Joy painted the cricket match at Christchurch in about 1850. The striped shirts and orderly concourse of the urban game contrasted with the rusticity of village cricket. The painting is also of topographical interest as it shows Priory Quay, Place Mill, Christchurch Priory and the Castle Keep, from meadows to the south-east.

Town cricket at Christchurch, painted by T.M. Joy in about 1850.

CYCLING

Ernest Clarke (foreground), *bugler and captain of Christchurch Bicycle Club, with members and their penny-farthing mounts in 1879.*

'Sociable' tricycle and riders from Christchurch, at the finger-post on Balmer Lawn – 7 miles from Beaulieu – in the 1880s.

Former watch-chain maker William Jeans, who designed and patented his own system of six gear-wheels, built tricycles at Christchurch. He rode one through a gale in October 1881, from Coventry to Bournemouth, in order to test the invention:

'I ran from Banbury to Oxford in a little under five hours, which is not so bad considering I had every now and then to heave the branches of trees out of the way, and I just escaped getting the bulk of an elm tree across my precious frame.'

Christchurch's other cycle manufacturer was Ernest Clarke. He came from Coventry, which was the cradle of the bicycle business, and established the Christchurch Bicycle Club. This flourished from 1876 to 1884 and had its club-room above Froud's boot and shoe depot on the corner of Church Street and Castle Street. Its success inspired the founding of a similar group in Poole, *The Christchurch Times* reported in 1877:

'Bicycle clubs are now established in most of the large towns throughout the country. Their object is to train members in the art of bicycle riding, to see that offences against the public are not wantonly committed by careless and indiscreet riding, and also to protect the members from the stupid treatment they sometimes receive from pedestrians, drivers and others, by whom their lives are occasionally imperilled.'

Their first long run, from the High Street to Salisbury on 2 June 1877, was notable for one such encounter, with the Hampshire Yeomanry. The militiamen brought their horses to a gallop and attempted to overtake the bicyclists on their last leg of the return journey, from Sopley to the High Street in Christchurch, 'but failed to do so, the riders of the wheeled machines being a little too good for them'.

Stephen Taylor from Milborne Port, splashing through the cobbled ford at Three Guinea Bridge, Sydling St Nicholas, in 1975.

DAIRYING

The classic Walter Pouncy shot of dairymaids (centre and right) *milking cows in Thomas Hardy's home parish of Stinsford, though by 1900 corrugated iron* (above the carts) *was as common as pantiles* (far left).

Above: *Milk churns in the porch of the White Horse Inn, Hinton St Mary, with landlord Harry Chinn (1864–1929) bearing the yoke and accompanied by grandson William John Chinn in 1904.*

Left: *Unidentified smallholders from Colehill in the 1890s, well endowed with the Puritan work ethic.*

Back in 1982 I tried to remind the public that not all Dorset cows were black-and-white. The horns on which to hang this story, figuratively and metaphorically, came with the herd of sixty Red Devon cattle at Kingston Lacy which were the pride and joy of their last private owner, Ralph Bankes, who died the previous year. He left them to the care of the National Trust, as part of its greatest ever bequest, which included 16,000 acres of real estate plus an equally valuable art collection.

Grazing beneath parkland cedars at Pamphill they were, to me, Thomas Hardy's cows. These were the last of the local free-range representatives of the traditional brown and off-yellow types of the Wessex novels. In the popular mind, however, the perception of Hardy's cows is very different.

John Schlesinger saw to that in 1966 with his film *Far from the Madding Crowd*. Since then the ubiquitous Friesian has had no contest from other breeds and can be seen in hundreds from downland viewpoints. Apart from around Kingston Lacy, that is, as the National Trust has maintained and expanded the Red Devon herd, which also does its share of conservation grazing around the prehistoric banks of Badbury Rings, and can be taken home in prime cuts from the butcher's slab in Wimborne.

Following their pedigrees backwards, I found that Revd William Dampier, farming in the Isle of Purbeck during the Napoleonic Wars, was disappointed that fellow stock-breeders spurned the opportunity to improve their mixed long-horned stock. They resisted the spread of the Devonshire breed which had been adopted by Lord Digby at Sherborne and Mr Wood at Osmington who proved that higher stocking numbers could be achieved and that they were just as hardy as existing breeds. Both landowners also found they were better for working ability, milk yield, and then butchery.

Their breeding animals had come from Devon but the Pope family, at Toller Whelme near Corscombe, could claim a similar herd which descended from those brought to Dorset by Ezekiel Pope (1673–1735) and which would remain on the family's land until 1884. Father and son continued the development of the herd, with John Pope (1718–94) and William Pope (1752–1831) maintaining the status quo, and the next William Pope (1800–79) introducing new blood from the West Country, which more than restored their reputation. The North Devon breed was nicknamed Red Ruby by the time the Devon Cattle Breeders' Society was formed in 1884.

Many Dorset farmers still tended to be more interested in dairying than beef but the Blackmore Vale was substantially devoted to feeding stock for the table. Their renown at Smithfield, when the first of the fat Red Rubies reached London from Dorset, was that they were as good as anything from Devon and Somerset. Butchers acclaimed this as being the finest-grained beef in the kingdom.

Mr Bridge, from Winford near Bristol, used oxen as draught animals and bred the pure North Devon breed, These were excellent milkers and also showed a tendency to fatten. He claimed an average weekly yield of 5 pounds of butter per cow, at a time when the distribution and sale of liquid milk was restricted, to the immediate vicinity of dairies.

The Victorian William Pope achieved similar success with his dual-purpose Red Devon herd. His cows were also good milkers and had long proved hardy enough to survive in the abundant fresh-air of the hills above Beaminster – through a succession of hard winters – where the weather generally comes from the west to make its next high-ground sweep after Dartmoor. These hills can be both wet and cold.

What Pope noticed was this his cows tended to put on weight when they ceased to be viable milk producers. He decided to make more of this propensity by buying bulls from the Quartly, Merson and Davy beef herds in Devon and an occasional real heavy-weight from Taunton Deane, of the kind called Rubies, which sired prolific milkers and big beef stock. William Pope's bulls frequently went on the road to service herds across Dorset.

Pope's son, the Revd W.J. Pope, dispersed the herd and let the estate, but his tenant, John Dight, still had the descendants of his father's stock grazing downland at Toller Whelme in 1893.

Meanwhile, a further high-quality Devon herd, via Cricket St Thomas, had arrived with Mr Shelter at New Barn Farm, Abbotsbury, in 1830. Another batch were introduced from Exeter and described by stock-dealer Jonathan Neale as the 'best dozen cows I have ever seen together'. Shelter continued to bring pure-blood stock from Devon and used bulls from the Toller Whelme and Little Toller herds. Shelter's stock was dispersed in the 1870s, by which time the next Devon herd had been established at Bradford Peverell, duplicated by Mr Brook at Brimsmore, near Yeovil, where the Davy and Quartly pedigree was maintained. The Little Toller breed, kept by dairyman Mr Yeates at Toller Fratrum, was dispersed in 1876. Rubies continued to arrive from the Vale of Taunton and were credited with bolstering Dorset's reputation for butter which relied on sustained milk yields.

So many West Country bulls had been brought into Dorset by the 1890s that most of the county's herds were of virtually pure-blood Devon stock. James Sinclair described them approvingly:

'In those herds are cows of a capital dairy type, thoroughly useful and kindly feeders. They are usually let in dairies of 20, 25, 30, 60, 50 or larger dairies being most commonly divided and let to different dairymen, but sometimes a dairyman rents a plurality of dairies.'

This letting system was historic in the western counties. About all that had changed over the years was what G.E. Fussell described as 'the minor matter of rent per cow'. He noted that in 1853 it was between £8-10s.-0d. to £10. rising to between £12 and £13 in 1878. This would cover an allowance of grassland to go with each cow, ranging from one to three acres of pasture and a similar area of hay meadow. They grazed on the 'aftermath' of arable crops in the autumn.

Dairying rent ran for 12 months from Old Candlemas Day (regarded as being 13 February when sticking with the pre-1752 calendar). Some dairymen would negotiate a rebate for each cow that had not calved before Old Lady Day, and on each heifer that had not calved before May Day. The cow rent included buildings necessary for accommodating the stock and also provision of a house for the dairyman and his family.

Stockman Bert Bugden of Bayard Barn, Bincombe, was interviewed for the BBC wireless series 'Village on the Air' in 1948. 'I bin yer aight year cum April,' he said in broad Darzet. 'Don't matter if be Christmas or Easter stock 'ave to be zid to.'

The Jacobs family with milking stools and cans at Walford Farm, between Wimborne and Furzehill, in 1895.

Corfe Mullen Dairy, in the Square at Wimborne, in about 1902.

Left: *Milk pail and the daily round – home delivery, unpasteurised and unbottled, at Sturminster Newton in 1947.*

Below: *Friesians crossing the village street from Church Lane in Combe Keynes, heading into the farmyard for milking, in 1969.*

Milking time blocking the lane as it had from time immemorial, at White Mill Farm near Shapwick, in August 1985.

DEMOLITIONS

Above: *The disappearance of a familiar landmark with the demolition of the Royal Oak at Upwey, below Ridgeway Hill, in April 1968.*

Right: *Half-demolished coke-house at the Gas Works behind Poole Quay in the early 1970s, with a soccer graffito showing that the premiership remained in the same hands for a generation.*

Dorset saw much of the bulldozer in the twentieth century, with post-war clearances removing more of Georgian Poole than had been devastated by German bombers, and we have also seen the disappearance of traditional industrial buildings. The latter included the levelling of an extensive coal-gas making plant behind what is now Dolphin Quay at Poole, the coming and going of the Central Electricity Generating Board's power station at Hamworthy, and mass removal of heathland pottery and brick-making kilns and yards.

EDUCATION

'Rushes O' with Miss Mary Elizabeth Bint and a basketry class for Edwardian boys at Blandford St Mary.

Return to school, at Leigh, for the parish council and reporter Rodney Legg (top left)*, as the candle flickers out* (centre) *on what will be the final bid at a hay-cutting auction in 1974.*

State schooling became compulsory in the twentieth century. Its introduction, though the Elementary Education Act of 1870, was due to the efforts of William Forster (1818–86) who was born in Bradpole. His home, Forsters, stands in what is now known as Forster's Lane, on the eastern side of the village. The Member of Parliament for Bradford, from 1861, he had a lucky life in politics, considering he received the Gladstone Government's poison chalice in 1880, as Secretary of State for Ireland. The following year that position made him the prime target for the Phoenix Park assassins, but Forster had resigned two days earlier, and as a result two replacements were stabbed to death.

EVENTS

Dedication of the Hansford Clock in the Borough Gardens, Dorchester, on its gift to the town by Charles Hansford in 1905.

Dairyman Farwell with 'Daisy' – William Henry Bond's best Devon cow from Tyneham – at Dorchester Agricultural Show, held in fields behind Icen Way in 1906.

Tree struck by lightning, toppled and splintered, at Glanvilles Wootton, on 14 April 1907.

Maypole in 1909 at Glanvilles Wootton, mainly for the girls, but 'Sidney is amongst them,' Mrs M. Meaden wrote to her friend Miss Cluett in Lydlinch.

Recreational grief, led by the brass band of the Dorset Constabulary, for the funeral of G.G. Palmer, en route from Weymouth to the cemetery in 1910.

The Square at Wimborne, looking across to the Crown Hotel (top left), during an election meeting for the general election of 1910 in which Henry Guest from Canford House – for the Liberal Party – narrowly took East Dorset against Conservative candidate Colonel Nicholson.

Left: Mothers' Union members from across Dorset, pausing for a cup of tea, during a gathering at Weymouth in 1921.

Below: From a Bournemouth collection, featuring an unknown Catholic family who may well be from a town far away, at a wedding given a Girl Guide guard of honour in 1922.

Scoutmaster Wilfred Brymer of Ilsington House and assistant Ray Stephens with Puddletown boys in 1930.

Villagers at Okeford Fitzpaine dressed as a 'Gypsy troop', collecting for hospitals, at the introduction of the National Health Service in 1947.

Runner Charles Bennett, from Shapwick was the first Briton to win Olympic gold by setting a 1500-metre world record in July 1900.

By just a fraction of a second, Roger Bannister swept to fame in 1954, as he registered the first sub-four minute mile in 1954. His achievement followed in the footsteps of almost totally forgotten Dorset athlete who more than half a century before had become the first Briton to win Olympic gold. As with Sir Roger Bannister, Charles Bennett (1874–1948) was unprepossessing in size, and on finding his photograph I recalled Bannister's self-depracating words about his own stature. 'You, sir, are too thin to be a runner,' a groundsman authoratively told him as he trained in Oxford.

In fact the wiry carry off medals in this game. Optimum lightness is vital for maximising motion from bursts of extreme energy. They may lack the stamina for marathon running but momentary movement is quite another matter, as Bennett proved by setting a 1500-metre world record in July 1900.

The Olympic event took place on grass in the Racing Club of France grounds in Paris and his speed was 4 minutes 6.2 seconds. That Sunday, on the same track, he then went on to take the 5000 metre record with a speed of 15 minutes 20 seconds. It was a duel with Frenchman Henri Deloge and cynics said that neither would have had a chance but for the date. The favourite, John Cregan from the United States, withdrew in protest at being asked to run on the Sabbath.

Charles Bennett, who already held a number of British records, was born in Shapwick. His father, Charles Henry

Bennett, was one of the village shopkeepers. In commercial terms he came second to the wonderfully named Pharaoh Feltham who was blacksmith, grocer and postmaster. George and Louisa Frampton were also retailers in Shapwick and James Guy was the landlord at the Anchor Inn.

A descendant of Thomas Davis Joyce, the farmer at White Mill, told me that her great-grandfather remembered 'boy Bennett running as if his life depended on it'. His chosen sprint, along flat ground beside the Stour meadows, was south-eastwards from West Street, Kings Farm and Steward's Lane, along Mill Lane, to the next road junction after Piccadilly Lane. This was the Drove which happens to be a mile from the Anchor.

These were the days of amateur athletics. Charles Bennett became an engine driver for the London and South Western Railway, between Weymouth and Waterloo. This gave him the opportunity to live and train in London, with the Finchley Harriers, and he retired to Bournemouth. He lived at West Howe and is buried in Kinson cemetery.

His grave was discovered by his grandson, Chris Bennett, in time for the Sydney Olympics of 2000 though the family had lost contact with the whereabouts of Charles Bennett's medals. The Bennett Centenary Mile was run at Shapwick that year.

FAIRS

At the fair, showing the setting up of the coconut shy (foreground) *on Woodbury Hill, Bere Regis, with an Iron Age rampart* (background) *in 1900.*

Above left: *September fair and the buildings of Woodbury Hill Farm, above Bere Regis, in 1900.*

Above: *Roundabout* (top left) *and stalls at Woodbury Hill Fair, Bere Regis, in the 1930s.*

Left: *Stock was still important at the first post-war Yetminster Fair on 17 April 1946.*

Yetminster Fair, as revived in the summer of 1976, took on a leisurely look.

As immortalised in the works of Thomas Hardy, traditional country fairs were best represented by that held on Woodbury Hill, above Bere Regis. This was associated with an anchoret's chapel and nearby sacred well which attracted pilgrims on 21 September each year to drink the healing water. As early as the reign of Henry III, in 1231, the week in which 21 September fell was that of Woodbury Hill Fair.

Being of vital importance to the economy, both for trade and to meet and 'hire' prospective employees, the right to hold a fair was on a par with that to have a market, being granted by the Crown and limited by statute. Unlike markets, fair grounds tended to be on what was regarded as neutral ground, devoid of a standing population, in a conspicuous location beside a major highway. The deserted earthworks of the Wessex hill-forts, such as Lambert's Castle, Poundbury Camp, Woodbury Hill and Yarnbury Castle, were convenient compounds for stalls and enclosures on these special occasions.

That on Woodbury Hill became a five-day event. Monday was Wholesale Day in which traders set up their stalls and began by buying and selling amongst themselves. Tuesday was Gentlefolk's Day in which the more restrained entertainments took place and huge quantities of oysters were consumed. Wednesday was Allfolks Day in which popular entertainments held sway. Thursday was Sheepfair Day in which sheep were the principal livestock – with numbers in excess of 10,000 head – but other pens included cattle and horses. Friday was Pack and Penny Day when the hilltop was cleared and disposals of unsold merchandise were at bargain prices.

By 1938, trading had ceased and only the two days of entertainments continued, but a year later these had to be cancelled and remained suspended for the duration of the Second World War. The fair struggled on through the years of austerity but 1951, when the Festival of Britain inspired new aspirations, saw its finale.

'Refreshing milk' was the slogan on the apron, at Yetminster Fair, on 10 July 1976.

FAMILIES

Colonel William Ernest Brymer (1840–1909) of Ilsington House, Puddletown, was the Member of Parliament for Dorchester and South Dorset for three decades.

Early photograph of William Henry Bond (1853–1935) who owned Tyneham House from 1898.

William Henry Bond (left) supervising the moving of a water-trough in the pasture between Tyneham Farm (background left) and Gad Cliff, in 1909.

Miss Margaret Bond – born in 1892 – was the youngest daughter of Mary and William Bond of Tyneham House.

Mary Bond (left), with her nieces Helen and Violet Meysey-Thompson, and daughter Lilian Bond on the lawn beside Tyneham House.

Left: *Margaret Bond and Grip beside the Elizabethan porch at Tyneham House.*

Below: *Sir Randolf Littlehales Baker MP (right) entertaining the Bond family at Ranston, Shroton, in 1907.*

Bottom left: *Editha Pomeroy, in a crinoline of about 1880, became Mrs John Bond of Tyneham House.*

Bottom right: *Mary Bond with mink stole and her basket, between daisies and rhododendrons at Tyneham.*

Above left: *Mary Bond and doves on the lawn at Tyneham House.*

Above: *Marjorie Phyllis Blake (left), Phyllis Watson-Smyth, brother Teddy Watson-Smyth, and Margaret Bond at Broad Bench, Tyneham, in 1902.*

Left: *Margaret Bond beside a rambling rose in the walled garden at Tyneham House in 1903.*

Margaret Bond in the donkey cart at the front door of Tyneham Rectory in 1904.

Above: *Violet Meysey-Thompson* (left) *and cousin Lilian Bond with a dead tern they found at Rempstone Gull Pond, near Corfe Castle, in 1904.*

Right: *Margaret Bond, beside the Elizabethan porch to the east front of Tyneham House, about to set off as the 'hare' in a paper-chase, 1905.*

Marjorie Blake (left), *Winnie Blake, Lilian Bond and Margaret Bond at Tyneham in 1905.*

Lilian Bond (left), *sister Margaret Bond and Fidget at Worbarrow Bay, Tyneham, in 1906.*

Lilian Bond in the walled garden at Tyneham House in 1909.

Tinge Whitnall (left) *and Mrs Whitnall with Lilian Bond holding her head in her hand* (right) *at Ranston, Shroton, in 1908.*

Margaret Bond in 1912.

Mary Bond with grandchildren Mary and John beside the south side of Tyneham House.

Mary Bond in the summer house at Tyneham in 1920.

Right: *Mary Bond of Tyneham House, looking serious in her passport picture for Norway, 1937.*

Below: *Algernon Bond* (left) *saying goodbye to fisherman Henry Miller before leaving Tyneham for the last time, to death in India.*

Below right: *Ralph Bond, the last private owner of Tyneham House, in 1920.*

Left: *Mrs John Henry Citchell and her sons beside ivy-clad Berwick, near Swyre, in 1910.*

Below: *Michael Rogers and Michael Rose playing pirates on the lawn at Okeford Fitzpaine Rectory in 1947.*

Many of these pictures have come from the Bond family at Tyneham. They typify the life of an English country squire in Victorian and Edwardian times. William Henry Bond, born at South Petherton, Somerset, in 1855, was the son of the Prebendary Henry Bond. In 1878, William Henry Bond married Mary Caroline Meysey-Thompson in London at Little St Marylebone Church. He inherited Tyneham House from an uncle in 1898 and lived there until his death in 1935.

Mary was the daughter of Sir Harry Stephen Meysey-Thompson. Mary's elder brother was Henry Meysey Meysey-Thompson, 1st Baron Knaresborough (1845–1929), a Liberal Unionist MP from 1880 to 1906. Her other distinguished brother was Colonel Richard Meysey-Thompson (1847–1826) of Nunthorpe Court, York, who received the medal of the Royal Humane Society for life-saving during the disaster at Newby Bridge in 1868.

William Henry Bond's uncle, Revd John Bond, lived at Tyneham until his death in 1898. In old age, he had a low-hung donkey-cart specially designed to prolong his mobility. John Bond was credited with having made Good Friday a conditional holiday for estate workers. Provided they attended church, in the morning, they could then spend the afternoon planting their own potatoes.

The first son of William Henry Bond was Algernon (Algy), a natural horseman, who joined the Eton Volunteers. Also an experienced boatman, he achieved almost legendary status among the old sea-salts from the Miller family of Worbarrow and Lulworth. Having crossed to Weymouth with boatman Henry Miller, to pick up a refitted boat, they were capsized by a squall as they returned into Worbarrow Bay. Algy could easily have swum to the shore, but Henry could not swim, so the pair of them clung to the hull. Fortunately their plight

had been witnessed, but by the time a small armada of rescue vessels had reached them both were half-drowned and suffering from hypothermia.

The women of Worbarrow had taken over the Coast Guard Station and prepared fires and blankets. Algy, almost dead from exhaustion and exposure, was brought back to life by the women rubbing scotch whisky into his body. One male onlooker was sure he had died and ran a mile up the valley to deliver the news to Tyneham House. 'Master Algy's drowned!' he gasped, as he fainted on the kitchen floor.

After this, Mary Bond offered swimming prizes, but only the boys from the Coast Guard Station competed. The view of the fishing families was that 'there's no back door to the sea'. They refused to learn to swim and were adamant that it was safer to stay with one's boat, in the hope of rescue, rather than chance the waves. If the vessel did break up, it was better to drown quickly, rather than fight the elements.

Mary Bond was no mean sailor. On one particularly atrocious voyage, from Malta to Marseilles, she was one of only three passengers who had the stomach to dine their way through the gale. Her two companions were a French admiral and his British equivalent, Sir Rosslyn Erskine Wemyss, but the latter eventually made his excuses. Mary, her daughter Lilian recalled, 'was left to uphold the honour of our British seamanship alone'.

Algernon Bond volunteered for service against the Boers and sailed for the South African War. He was maimed by injuries sustained during the attack on Surprise Hill during the siege of Ladysmith but survived to return as a hero in a homecoming which saw him being carried by the crowd through Wareham. Villagers at Tyneham upstaged this welcome by erecting a triumphal arch. Algy's thankful parents also marked his survival by donating a pipe organ to replace the harmonium in Tyneham Church. Comprising two barrels, each with eight sets of rotating staples, it has since been moved to Steeple Church.

Algy went off again, however, on his next adventure. This was to India where he succumbed to cerebral malaria.

The second son and heir of William Henry Bond was William Ralph Garneys Bond (1880–1952). Born at Fryern Court, Fordingbridge, Hampshire, he was wiry, non-sporting apart from swimming and rowing, and suffered a near-fatal bout of pneumonia which left him with a cough for the rest of his life. Ralph was the artistic member of the family who collected and studied specimens of Purbeck wildlife. In 1897 he was awarded the medal of the Royal Humane Society for jumping into the River Thames to save the life of a struggling and drunken Guardsman.

From the turn of the century Ralph's great friend at New College, Oxford, was Walter Guinness. They went off together in January 1901 on a tour of the entire northern hemisphere including Germany, Russia, Siberia, China, Japan and Canada. Bond and Guinness were among the first westerners to cross Asia on the newly-opened Trans-Siberian Railway, a journey of eleven days which included a voyage in the Baikal steamer.

Ralph married Evelyn Isabel Blake from Danesbury, Hertfordshire, in 1920. He was on home leave from the Sudan Political Service. There he shot a Dorcas gazelle of world-record size in 1913 and was the governor of Fung province, and then Dongola, until retirement in 1926. Said, his loyal servant from boyhood, remained with him throughout the career. Menageries at Tyneham were outclassed by a Sudanese zoo which followed him around and in one case, namely Maudie the giraffe, came home with him to London Zoo.

Evelyn Blake's father was Colonel Arthur Maurice Blake of the Grenadier Guards and the 1st Volunteer Battalion, the Bedfordshire Regiment, who married Isabella Crawley in 1881.

Ralph Bond's son and heir, Mark Bond who was born in 1922, never inherited the family estate around Tyneham House in the Isle of Purbeck. The entire 3003-acre parish had been requisitioned for a massive expansion of the Lulworth tank gunnery ranges, six days before Christmas in 1943.

Ralph's sister Lilian M. Garneys Bond (1887–1980) married her cousin Ivo Bond, from the neighbouring mansion on the other side of the Purbeck Hills, in the summer of 1914. Ivo was the son of Nathaniel Bond of Creech Grange who had married Lady Selina Jane Scott from Encombe. After the evacuation, living in No. 1 Queen's Avenue, Dorchester, Mrs Bond recalled her village idyll for *Tyneham: a Lost Heritage* which was published in the town by Henry Longman in 1956 and became the county's best loved book.

The cast-list, with potted descriptions condensed from Lilian Bond's writings but failing to do justice to her characterful vignettes, included:

Amos (talkative Aberdeen terrier who was the Bond family's favourite gun dog)

Henry George Balson (killed in the Great War)

Old Balson (wiry woodsman, gnarled as a tree-root)

Mrs Barnes (Postmistress from 1911 when widow Mrs Pitman moved to Worbarrow to marry fisherman Joseph Miller)

Blitz (impetuous trotting donkey)

Cicely Garneys Bond (Lilian's elder sister, who married Lewys Legg Yeatman, in 1910)

Herbert Ivo de Kenton Bond (Lilian's cousin at Creech Grange, who she married in 1914)

John Wentworth Garneys Bond (1865–1948; barrister and clerk in the House of Commons until retirement in 1926; Lilian Bond's cousin and brother-in-law from Creech Grange)

Margaret H. Garneys Bond (Lilian's younger sister, Margot, born 1892)

Laurence Burt (of Povington, killed in the Great War)

Henry Charles (pensioner; had worked for rector Revd C. S. Homan)

Charles Job Cleall (killed in the Great War)

James Curtis (head gardener)

Daniel (Aberdeen terrier)

Grace Draper (wife of Warwick Draper of Sheepleaze, Worbarrow)

Christopher Draper (Christo, the younger son of Grace and Warwick Draper)

Mary Draper (daughter of Grace and Warwick Draper)

Philip Draper (elder son of Grace and Warwick Draper)

Warwick Draper (London barrister, built Sheepleaze on cliffs at Worbarrow in 1911)

Maggie Drew (kitchen-maid who prepared Tyneham's protesting felines for their annual visit to the Boxing Day cat and poultry show at Corfe Castle)

Henry Ford (from Steeple Leaze, killed in the Great War while serving with Canadian forces)

Mrs Fry (schoolmistress; suffered chronic arthritis; eventually followed her adopted daughter to Canada)

Goliath (pet polecat ferret with silver undercoat, who answered to his name and was taken out on a lead)

(?) Gostling (district nurse, based at Tyneham)

Frank Gould (of Povington, killed in the Great War)

Tom Gould (under-gardener and then sole gardener for more that four decades, who married Virtue Everitt and fought at Chitral and with the Dorsetshire Regiment throughout the Great War. 'Tom had a splendid head with strong and clear-cut features full of character, and would have made the perfect model for a militant saint.' They lived in Gardener's Cottage, built by 'Uncle' John Bond, which was the newest building in the village)

Old Gover (cottager from East Creech who tended South Egliston garden and its Gwyle; organist to Creech Grange and Steeple churches)

Philip Harvell (Mrs Joseph Tizzard's crippled brother)

Harry Holland (of Baltington Farm, killed in the Great War)

John Holland (of Baltington Farm, killed in the Great War)

Lieutenant C. K. Homan (rector's son serving in 6th Battalion, Dorsetshire Regiment, killed on the Somme, 18 September 1915)

Revd Claude S. Homan (rector from 1897 to 1913, married May Digby from Studland Manor)

Miss Hester Mary Hull (ran Tyneham Farm after departure of Joseph Hull)

James Hull (Victorian tenant of Baltington Farm; moved to Higher Kingston Farm, Stinsford)

Joseph Hull (brother of James; Victorian tenant of Tyneham Farm)

Frederick Knight (coachman, who drove the station brougham and pair, lived in the former Museum in Tyneham House grounds, for fifteen years)

Stephen Lillington (of Povington, killed in the Great War)

(?) Lucas (shepherd)

Sophie McLellan (succeeded Ada Newman as lady's maid; soft-spoken Scottish dressmaker; distinctive heart-shaped face with widely parted big eyes)

Charlie Meech (odd job man)

William George Meech (gamekeeper at Tyneham, killed in the Great War)

Charles Miller (fisherman, lived at Fern Hollow, Worbarrow. Brother of Joseph. Both had similar strikingly dark features with Charlie being distinguished by a black beard)

Jack Miller (fisherman at Worbarrow, with blue eyes and fair hair. He married Miggie – otherwise Alice White Rose – who was the cook from the Royal Victoria Hotel at Swanage where Jack had driven a horse-drawn omnibus. They moved into Sea Cottage on the death of Joseph)

Joseph Miller (Joe, a handsome fisherman with sideburns, was the brother of Charles. He lived at Sea Cottage. Second wife was the village postmistress, Mrs Pitman – nee Tizzard – whom he married in 1910)

Henry Miller (cousin of Charles and Joseph, lived at Hill Cottage, Worbarrow, with wife Louisa and their unmarried son, Tom)

Rose Miller (Granny Miller, mother of Miggie, of Sea Cottage, Worbarrow)

Sydney Mills (coachman)

Louie Milsome (adopted daughter of Mrs Fry, the schoolmistress; married Charlie Tizzard and emigrated to Saskatchewan)

Beatrice Mintern (daughter of Tommy and Sarah Mintern)

Rose Mintern (daughter of Tommy and Sarah Mintern)

Thomas Mintern (Tommy, boatman and smallholder at Worbarrow, married to Sarah)

Willie Mintern (sixteen-year-old only son of the Minterns, drowned with a boy from London, while on a fishing trip off Worbarrow Tout on 16 June 1923; Willie's body was washed ashore several weeks later)

Winnie Mintern (daughter of Tommy and Sarah Mintern)

Ada Newman (nursery maid and then Mrs Bond's lady's maid; left on becoming Mrs Dell)

Mores family (ran Victorian village shop; during their time it operated a bakery)

Mrs Pitman (Postmistress; sister of the Tizzard brothers, married Joseph Miller in 1911)

Emily Pink Rose (sister of Alice White Rose at Worbarrow)

Mary Rose (mistress at Tyneham School, circa 1890)

(?) Sansom (shepherd; father of disabled Jessie)

Tarry Samways (partner of Thomas Mintern)

Walter Smith (farmer, at Tyneham Farm)

Anna Petrovna Sokolova (Russo-Prussian governess, known as 'Socky')

Isabella Summers ('strictly methodical' housemaid from Winfrith who ran the Tyneham House pantry. Retired to Dorchester but returned to cover staff absences)

Arthur Taylor (killed in the Palestine campaign of 1918, buried on the Mount of Olives)

Bert Taylor (killed in the Great War)

William Taylor (parish clerk, sexton and woodsman, who took over from Old Balson)

Harriet White (schoolmistress at Tyneham, from Kingston, who married Charles Miller, sang in the church choir for four decades and celebrated their golden wedding at Worbarrow)

Alfred Tizzard (fence-maker, hedger and ditcher)

Charlie Tizzard (youngest brother, carters' boy)

George Tizzard (brother, carter)

William Tizzard (brother, carter)

Eleanor Truell (rector's daughter, played the harmonium in Tyneham Church)

Revd William Truell (curate in charge at Tyneham during the incumbency of his brother-in-law, Revd Nathaniel Bond of Creech Grange)

John Weeks (bearded ex-Navy chief officer of Worbarrow Coast Guard Station)

Bert Wickerson (chief boatman at the Coast Guard Station, Worbarrow, who married the chief housemaid from Tyneham House)

William Woadden (butler and brewer at Tyneham House)

Miss Norah Woodman (mistress at Tyneham School in Edwardian times; church organist)

Revd Christopher Wordsworth (rector from 1889 to 1895, who was lacking in private means, which meant that his wife, Reeve, walked with the female villagers to Wareham each week with a perambulator to collect household shopping)

Lewys Legg Yeatman (who married Cicely Bond, in 1910, was the son of the Bishop of Worcester, the Right Revd Huyshe Wolcott Yeatman-Biggs of Hartlebury Castle, Kidderminster)

Because of its fate, more than can be said for anywhere else in Dorset, Tyneham and its former ruling family belong to a lost world. Even its renowned fan-palm became a memory in the middle of the war. This specimen of *Chaemoerops fortuneii* was decapitated by WAAFs stationed in Tyneham House, for Christmas decorations at RAF Brandy Bay which was a coastal radar station, in 1942.

The Lower Road to Worbarrow, which followed the Gwyle stream, was replaced by the straight Admiralty Road to the Coast Guard Station in the nineteenth century. Another lost road was Shoemaker's Lane, leading towards Upper Horse Close and the coastal ridge above Egliston, which crossed the Avenue east of Tyneham House. It was named with irony for the damage its rough stones caused to footwear. The Coffin Tree on the parish boundary at the top of the Purbeck Hills took its name for the shape of a coffin on the trunk, marking a suicide burial there. The victim, a milkmaid, had hanged herself in the cow-stalls at Baltington Farm.

Fishing

Night fishing off the southern shore of Poole Harbour in 1907.

Romany fish-woman offering a prime plaice at Burton Bradstock in 1900.

Worth Matravers fisherman setting off with his pots in 1907.

The further one goes back the more important fishing from Dorset becomes, for half a millennium, to the harvesting of vast fish stocks on the other side of the Atlantic when the fishing fleet from Poole was catching cod on the Grand Banks off Newfoundland. In home waters, the mackerel appeared in shoals, and were pulled ashore in their thousands in loops of net that were hand-hauled on to the Chesil Beach.

In recent times, Dorset has been best known for its shellfish, particularly lobsters, crabs and scallops. Sporting catches of fish became more important as commercial prospects declined. As the natural world lost its stocks, Dorset's plentiful crop of twentieth-century shipwrecks became locally important as artificial reefs, providing a man-made refuge for species ranging from bass to conger eel.

Fishermen raising a lobster-pot off Seacombe at Worth Matravers.

FLOODS

Looking from Hammoon towards Manston, with the River Stour in full flood over the top of its bridge (centre), *in 1947.*

Rodney Legg (bottom left) *beside Longham Bridge, inches above the River Stour in the autumn floods of 1958.*

Taking a drive to see the Stour in flood used to be a regular leisure activity in Bournemouth suburbia. Floods were our equivalent of natural disasters, which mostly inundated the meadows though occasionally the waters swept through Blandford as well as threatening Wimborne.

One such trip, on 5 October 1958, took in Holdenhurst, Throop, Longham and Hampreston with water as far as you could see, before the cutting of a straight channel between Muccleshell and Hurn Court bypassed the bottleneck at Throop Mill. Towards Bournemouth and the sea, the Stour was always wide, but even the upper reaches around Sturminster Newton could compete after a few days of heavy rain. Most of the water that poured across Bournemouth's green belt was secondhand rainfall from the Blackmore Vale.

There I nearly lost my quite new Vauxhall Astra in a flash flood, late one night in 2000/01, as the roads became canals. Around the corner an elderly driver lost his life as the River Divelish, living up to its name by turning into a torrent, carried his vehicle away from a ford at Fifehead Neville and jammed it between the supports of a farm bridge near Plumber Manor. My engine recovered, despite cutting out, and I had to struggle to turn on a narrow lane between high banks in rising water. Daylight revealed clumps of grass protruding from the radiator and light fittings.

GARDENS

Stone steps between the conifers at Downhayes, Langton Matravers, in 1907.

Yuccas in flower, along the south side of the grounds of Tyneham House, in 1910.

Right: *Tyneham House and the yuccas, looking northward to the drive, in its final peacetime summer of 1939.*

Below: *Yucca and pond, in a view westwards beside the south-east corner of Tyneham House in 1905.*

Henry Charles of Rectory Cottages, in the garden of Tyneham Rectory, in 1909.

The famous Wessex gardens, visited each spring by coachloads of Dutch admirers, are mostly across the county boundary in Somerset and Wiltshire. The great exception is Abbotsbury Sub Tropical Gardens, in the micro-climate of a sheltered hollow behind the Chesil Beach. Tyneham could boast something similar, though on a much smaller scale, with mild sea coast temperatures and humidity allowing the survival of exotic plants.

Dorset gardens tend to be under-stated. The best merge their borders and prizes – the introduced rarities – with wilder patches of native vegetation which are treated with equal pride. Snowdrops emerge from the leaf-litter in mid-winter where foxgloves will hold the breeze in high summer. The same eclectic mix applies to the shrubs and trees. That jigsaw makes for perfection.

One of the greatest of plant artists who travelled the globe, Miss Marianne North who has a gallery of 832 botanical paintings on permanent display at Kew Gardens, expressed that view when she found her vision of Eden, for the purposes of retirement in 'a garden with a cottage' in the Cotswolds. There, in 1886, she wrote an appreciation of the English flora that also remains valid across Dorset from the Marshwood Vale to Purbeck:

'No life is so charming as a country one in England, and no flowers are sweeter or more lovely than the primroses, cowslips, bluebells, and violets which grow in abundance around me here.'

HARVEST

Left: *Cutting wheat at Langton Matravers in 1909.*

Below: *Harvesting at East Farm at Tolpuddle, farmed by Thomas King, in 1905.*

Bottom: *Steam engine powering a wheat thresher at Langton Matravers in 1909.*

The 'Advance' threshing machine restored to working life for one of the first big steam fairs, at Stourpaine Bushes, in the 1970s.

Horse-cart being loaded with sacks of wheat from a drystone wall at Blacklands, near Acton, in 1909.

Thomas Cozier's Sun Inn (left), at Morcombelake, with corn stooks on the slopes of Hardown Hill in about 1915.

Steam-powered threshing machines revolutionised the Victorian harvest but these belt-driven wooden boxes look like dinosaurs compared with what was to follow. The last threshing machine contractors in Dorset, hiring out machinery and services, were listed by *Kelly's Directory of Dorsetshire* in 1939:

John Farris and Sons Ltd, Belle Vue Engineering Works, Victoria Street, Shaftesbury.
Absolom William Field, Okeford Fitzpaine.
John Gifford, West Mill Iron Works, Dorchester.
Herbert Nelson Harris, St Michael's Foundry, Bridport.
Stanley Osmond, Stafford Farm, West Stafford.

The post-war ascendancy of the combine harvester has fully automated the harvest. Even the straw has gone through an evolution in form and shape, from stook to bale, and now is shrink-wrapped in industrial strength green plastic to resemble Swiss rolls.

What little is left on the ground is no longer gleaned by country folk. There is neither the economic imperative or cultural background that compels people to salvage such waste. It was a communal right of access to the fields that went back to time immemorial. Perhaps the equipment has become so efficient that nothing now falls to the ground but the herds of roe deep that spread out across the stubble seem to be finding something of interest.

Margery, Vera and Olive from Hammoon, gleaning to the backdrop of Hambledon Hill, in 1948.

Flower gathering in a lush meadow beside Barnes Orchard, Bagber, near Sturminster Newton, to mark the centenary of the birth of the parson-poet William Barnes in 1901.

Left: *George Ayles from Colehill sharpening his scythe with a whetting-stone in 1900.*

Below: *Pitchfork and scythe with Mr Beavis wearing the moleskin trousers* (right), *in a two-pronged effort to gather the hay in quarrying country at Langton Matravers in 1909.*

Beavis scything on the stone plateau at Langton Matravers in 1909.

Horse mowing of a larger meadow at Coombe, Langton Matravers, in 1909.

Above: *Semi-mechanised methods entering their final era, with a horse-drawn reaper beside Leigh Common, Colehill, in 1901.*

Left: *Mowing the hay on Pentridge Farm, near the birthplace of parson poet William Barnes, at Bagber in the heart of the Blackmore Vale.*

Seventeen-year-old Mary Trowbridge, at Pentridge Farm, near Sturminster Newton, in her Edwardian bonnet.

At home on the range, in Dorchester photographer Walter Pouncy's version of Constable's haywain, shot at West Stafford in 1901.

Collecting the cut in the final stage of haymaking at Coombe, Langton Matravers, in 1909.

Cart and elevator, plus an iconic white horse, rick-building at Coombe, Langton Matravers, in 1909.

Final days of horse-drawn haymaking, near Worth Matravers, in the hot summer of 1959.

Hand-moving a meadow has become a lost art, as has using the whetstone, but this used to be a familiar countryside ballet. Gangs of workers performed the rhythm of the scythe with shining blades that took the top cut but left thick swathes of grazing grass. Hand techniques could be applied selectively, for precise applications, in a way that was difficult for horse-drawn alternatives and impossible with modern mechanised methods. Scything could cut the way to the binder, floor patches of nettles, docks and thistles, or recover swirls of wind-battered corn.

Use of the scythe was a skill, being far from easy as C.F. Snow pointed out in 1949, because it was much more taxing than it looked. Far from being tireless and automatic, its application would begin with the uninitiated finding that the implement had a natural disposition for alternatively stabbing the ground and then sailing skywards over the vegetation it was meant to be cutting.

With the novice performer, the blade would come and go – broken, replaced or sharpened – before realisation that the key to its delivery was to adjust to one's snead. That was the handle. Overcoming its inherent awkwardness turns the previously cumbersome tool into a precious possession to treasure for life.

You tested the setting of the blade (which did get replaced) by stretching your hand towards the point whilst keeping the butt end against your chin. Adjust the position of the blade so that your thumb just touches its tip. Then go into the field and begin the learning curve, following Snow's instructions:

'To avoid the digging-in movement and the high swing, stand with the feet slightly apart, right foot forward. Begin the stroke with the right hand a little in front of the right leg. Then bring the right hand round to the left knee, keeping the blade horizontal to the ground. The heel of the blade should come into action at the beginning of the sweep, and the point at the end. The right hand takes the weight of the scythe and the left hand takes the pull.

'It is important not to hack the grass – a steady rhythmic movement is needed and this can only be achieved by practice. It is important not to hurry, too. As with so many other jobs which are done by country people, mowing may look slow to the uninitiated. But it is the slowness which conserves strength and allows men to work on, tireless through the long hours, when the workers who rush at their work are tired out and working spasmodically.'

HOME

The plight of the peasantry in Dorset, as drawn for The Illustrated London News *at Winterborne Whitechurch, in 1846.*

Left: *Comfortable and cosy Dorset living, as represented by future squire Ralph Bond's bedroom at the end of the nursery passage in Tyneham House, in 1902.*

Below: *Upper-class furnishings as represented in the ballroom at Bryanston House, rebuilt to Norman Shaw's designs by the 2nd Viscount Portman, between 1889 and 1894.*

Right: *The hall in the new Bryanston House in 1895.*

Below: *Portraits and books, in the library at Kingston Lacy House, bequeathed to the National Trust by Ralph Bankes on his death in 1981.*

Organ and dining table at Kingston Lacy House in 1982.

'The Judgment of Solomon' by Sebastiono del Piombo, among the most valuable in the entire National Trust collection, in Kingston Lacy House in 1985 before removal – and then replacement – of surrounding panelling.

Over-furnished, magnificently, the Spanish room at Kingston Lacy House embodies centuries of Bankes family taste and collecting.

That Brideshead Revisited *moment, captured in the bathroom at Kingston Lacy House, by photographer Colin Graham in August 1985.*

Left: *Author and historian Rodney Legg in the bathroom of Sherford Farm, near Morden Park Corner, in 1972.*

Below: *Horse brasses and a warming pan beside the historic open fireplace in the living room at Yeomans, Okeford Fitzpaine, in 1975.*

Dorset as a place of contrasts, at both ends of the social spectrum, became a national scandal, to the embarrassment of its gentry. The plight of the Dorset peasantry in the 'Hungry Forties' was exposed by two letter-writing clergymen. Henry Moule (1801–80) wrote from Fordington Vicarage, Dorchester, to Prince Albert as landlord of the Duchy of Cornwall and to the *Dorset County Chronicle*, while Lord Sidney Godolphin Osborne (1808–89), from Durweston Rectory, as 'S.G.O' was a regular correspondent in the columns of *The Times*. 'God will not have the poor oppressed in body or soul,' he thundered.

The wordsmith Thomas Carlyle produced this vivid vignette of Dorset's well-heeled caring clergyman:

'The strange Revd Lord Sidney, the famous S.G.O. of the newspapers, and one of the strangest brother mortals I ever met; a most lean, tall and perpendicular man, face palpably aristocratic but full of plebeian mobilities, free and easy rapidities, nice laughing little grey eyes, careless, honest, full of native ingenuity, sincerity, innocent vanity, incessant talk, anecdote, personal, distractedly speculative, oftenest purposely distracted, never altogether boring. To me his talk had one great property, it saved all task of talking on my part. He was very intrinsically polite too and we did very well together.'

Lord Sidney denounced his fellows in the landowning class for keeping their workers below the poverty line, as he discovered when he started calling at their homes:

'I found the woman with two of the children, eating a few unwholesome potatoes and some bread; a child of nine years of age dead in a coffin close to them; the only ascent to the bedroom by a broken ladder.'

George Bankes MP, from Kingston Lacy House, rallied spirited opposition in the House of Commons but only succeeded in drawing further attention to the seriousness of the situation. Lord Sidney won the hearts of the people but found himself ostracised by his peers, retiring to Lewes, Sussex, in 1875.

Within sight of his Dorset home stood the aristocratic pile of Bryanston House, the seat of the Berkeley-Portman family, which represented power and status, emerging from the Victorian era completely rebuilt. William Henry Berkeley, 2nd Viscount Portman (1829–1919) inherited the estate from his father in 1888 and set about demolishing its historic mansion which had been built by James Wyatt in 1778.

Its replacement, in red brick by Norman Shaw who is principally remembered for designing New Scotland Yard, became Bryanston School. The 2nd Viscount lived to be ninety, at the end of the First World War, but the family's hold on their Dorset lands slipped to the Crown Commissioners, as a result of death duties, after the next two successors – the 3rd and 4th Viscounts – died in the same decade, in 1923 and 1929. Elsewhere, such as across Marylebone and Mayfair, the name and wealth endured.

HORSES

For painters as well as photographers, Lyme Regis blacksmith Samuel Govier presented an irresistible image, immortalised as 'The Master Smith of Lyme Regis' by James Abbott McNeill Whistler in 1895.

Cicely Bond on 'Solomon' opening an evocative series of equestrian snap-shots from Edwardian Tyneham.

Cicely Bond (left), with Phyllis Watson-Smyth on 'Basket', on the lawn beside Tyneham House.

Cicely Bond (left), Lilian Bond on 'Blitz' the donkey, and Phyllis Watson-Smyth on 'Basket' at Tyneham.

Carriage horse 'Blaze' dropped dead on Grange Hill when Cicely Bond was driving.

'Palmer' posing in front of the brewhouse in the grounds of Tyneham House.

'Regina' at Tyneham.

Above: *'Castor' and 'Blitz' the donkey beside the wall at Tyneham Farm.*

Right: *Walter Smith, the farmer at Tyneham Farm, with 'Punch'.*

Margaret Bond on 'Punch'.

James Bond's saddlery in West Borough, Wimborne, with street busker 'Holy Joe' (left) on his accordion, in 1900.

To military men, the age of the horse ended with the cavalry charge of the Queen's Own Dorset Yeomanry at Agagia, on 26 November 1916. From it, in Tyneham House, the trophy was a Senussi sword captured by 'C' Squadron. Back on Purbeck's western coast the final generation of riding horses included Basket, Castor, Palmer, Punch, Regina and Solomon, with carriage horse Blaze and Blitz the donkey.

It is no contest when it comes to my favourite images of a blacksmith, both in photographs and on canvas, for Samuel Govier (1855–1934) provided American artist James Abbott McNeill Whistler (1834–1903) with his subject 'The Master Smith of Lyme Regis'. This hangs in Boston Museum. The 'Little Forge', as Whistler titled it in another work, was established above the Great House in Broad Street by George Govier. Ironically, it became Watson's Garage – founded by Jack Watson – until the site was redeveloped for a budget store, by F.W. Woolworth & Co Ltd.

The motor car and lorry had taken the place of the horse on the road and the tractor in the field. Ferguson and Ford were the new names on the land. 'Farm better, Farm faster, with Ferguson' was the slogan of Harry Ferguson Ltd whose tractors were manufactured by the Standard Motor Company in Coventry.

Blackmore Vale hounds meeting on the meadow beside Town Bridge, Sturminster Newton, to a backdrop of great elms in 1947.

Misty morning meet of the Blackmore Vale hounds, in the Courts of Sherborne School, early in the 1970s.

Horses retained their primacy in country sports, particularly for fox-hunting, in Dorset. Traditional scenes like this added a splash of colour and controversy until reduced to a truncated form of the pursuit by legislation in February 2005.

INDUSTRY

The workers of Bourton Foundry, which had produced the biggest mill-wheels ever made, in 1902.

Metal mill-wheels transformed the working of corn and cloth mills during the late nineteenth century. Most of those in Dorset and Somerset were made by Bourton Foundry which by the turn of the twentieth century employed more than 200 workers and during the Great War became a munitions factory producing the cases for Mills bombs, until disruption from nature rather than warfare when the works was washed out by a flood in 1917.

The main industrial zone in Dorset was around Poole which had several foundries. The principal iron-works was Dorset Iron Foundry in West Quay Road. Agricultural machinery makers Lott and Walne Ltd had their foundry in Dorchester. Herbert Nelson Harris operated St Michael's Foundry at Bridport; and Richard Cox and Son were at Ranelegh Road, Weymouth.

The heathlands from Poole to Wareham became a three dimensional landscape with the pits, kilns and chimneys of a string of extensive potteries which mass-produced tiles, drainage pipes and bricks for the new suburbia.

Sandford Pottery, typical of those on the heath between Wareham and Poole, derelict in 1972.

LORRIES

FX 414, William Bedford's watercress delivery lorry at Bere Regis in 1907, when he went into a partnership that turned the firm into Bedford and Dwight.

Sturminster Newton's principal haulage contractor, Harry Charles Turk, with lorry No. 10 in 1936.

Carriers became hauliers, via a flirtation with steam lorries, as heavy vehicles moved with the times and embraced the potential of the internal combustion engine. It was also an aspiration for larger businesses to acquire their own means of transport, for reasons both practical and prestigious, for advertising their two-digit telephone numbers was almost as important as fulfilling deliveries.

MANSIONS

Magnificent mediaeval leaded window over the porch at Forde Abbey, photographed by Edwin Dodshon on 12 July 1924.

Eagles flanking the entrance to Mapperton Manor House, the home of Henry Compton, in 1924.

The old Bryanston House, built by James Wyatt in 1778, seen a century later before demolition and replacement by the 2nd Viscount Portman in 1889.

Encombe, the home of John Scott, 3rd Earl of Eldon – set in the Golden Bowl on the Purbeck coast – looking northwards across its lake in 1918.

Tyneham House, from the garden to the south-east, featuring the older generation of Bonds – Thomas, Jane and Mary – in the 1880s.

The Elizabethan east front of Tyneham House, looking north-westwards from the slope below Tyneham Great Wood in 1909.

Dorset's collection of minor stately homes have a place in the landscape but despite their appearance of permanence there have been inevitable comings and goings. The James Wyatt Bryanston House failed to survive the nineteenth century and was replaced by what is now the Norman Shaw Bryanston School.

Lost mansions in the twentieth century include Turnworth House, which was the original for Thomas Hardy's Hintock House in *The Woodlanders*, and Tyneham House on the Purbeck coast. The latter, largely demolished in 1968 after having been requisitioned for the wartime expansion of the Lulworth Ranges, remains the saddest of the losses though its Elizabethan north porch went on to a new life, as the back door to Bingham's Melcombe House.

Families have also moved on, including Bankes from Kingston Lacy, Portman from Bryanston, and Scott and the Eldon title from Encombe. Aristocratic arrivals during the twentieth century were headed by Viscount Hinchingbrooke MP, to Mapperton Manor in the hills above Beaminster, who become the 10th Earl of Sandwich on succeeding his father in 1962 but disclaimed his peerages for life.

MILLS

West Mills, on the River Piddle at Wareham, in 1909.

West Mill, on the Corfe River below Corfe Castle, in 1909.

The Mill Pond at Swanage, looking south-eastwards up Church Hill, in 1909.

Stanbridge Mill, on the River Allen below Horton Inn, derelict in 1973.

Above: *Town Mill on Shreen Water in the centre of Gillingham, looking northwards from Town Bridge in 1973, was operated for many years by G.B. Matthews and Co. Ltd.*

Right: *Equipment at Powerstock Mill, West Milton, disused in 1973.*

Dorset's historic corn and fulling mills, which cleansed wool, suffered greatly in the twentieth century. Most of their machinery went for scrap and many of the buildings were demolished or converted into up-market dwellings. Very few, such as that at Sturminster Newton, remain intact and usable.

Picturesque losses in first half of the last century included both West Mill and Arfleet Mill at Corfe Castle. Buildings beside the Mill Pond at Swanage fared better, being either renovated or rebuilt, but Loud's Mill at Dorchester and the

Town Mill in Gillingham were less fortunate. The latter went through the full cycle of decline from vandalism and fires through to demolition and clearance.

Stanbridge Mill, near Horton, went through several stages of dereliction but then fell into the safety net of gentrification. West Mills at Wareham has also survived, though in a rather compromised location, as it is now sandwiched between the railway line and a bypass, built across the adjoining common land.

MOTORCYCLES

Aircraftsman Thomas Edward Shaw, otherwise known as Lawrence of Arabia, on RK 4907, from his series of Brough Superior motorcycles which became a familiar sight on Dorset roads until his fatal crash in May 1935.

J.P. Toms of Bere Regis, described as 'Britain's oldest motorcyclist', setting off at the age of eighty-four to ride from Swanage to Exeter in August 1936.

By 1914, the motorcycle had evolved into models such as the New Hudson and Triumph, starting with the 2.25 horse-power two stroke Junior Triumph which was basically a stretched bicycle frame that had an engine instead of pedals. From 1923 until his death after falling from a Brough Superior motorcycle in May 1935, national hero Lawrence of Arabia lived at Clouds Hill near Bovington Camp, and was a familiar figure speeding through the Dorset lanes.

An ageing contemporary, J.P. Toms who was born at Briantspuddle, lived in Bere Regis and was buried at Puddletown, also received headlines for his riding skills, being acclaimed as Britain's oldest motorcyclist when he rode from Swanage to Exeter at the age of eighty-four in August 1936.

Left: Press picture of veteran motorcyclist J.P. Toms, nicknamed 'King Dick', marked on the back in 1936 for use 'with story' and the instruction 'delete the reporter'.

Below: Vintage motorcycles at a rally in the grounds of Sherborne Castle in 1972.

The Theatre in the Larmer Grounds, opened to the public without charge by Lieutenant-General Augustus Pitt-Rivers, in 1898 when there were 40,712 visitors.

Cart ride to the polls from the Newton side of the river into Sturminster Newton, extolling 'Vote for Baker', in the 1910 general election.

Mrs Mary Bond (second left) *and family from Tyneham House below Rockleigh at Peveril Point, Swanage, on an incoming tide in 1903.*

Above: *Bus from Sturminster Newton (left) and a party of visitors on arrival at Osmington Mills, between the Coastguard Cottages (centre) and the Picnic Inn, in the 1950s.*

Left: *Portesham was visited by Sturminster Newton Sunday School in the hot summer of 1959.*

Tyneham visits Norway, aboard the Vandyck *in August 1937, with the passengers including Mrs Mary Bond (left) Miss Margaret Bond, Hugo du Plessis, Gerald du Plessis, Hyacinth du Plessis and Ann Yeatman.*

There is a delightful account of the provisions for Victorian picnickers in *A Short Guide to the Larmer Grounds, Rushmore; King John's House; and the Museum at Farnham, Dorset* by General Augustus Pitt-Rivers (1827–1900). This hard-backed title, in dark blue buckram to match his archaeological volumes, dates from only months before his death. Written in the third person, it shows how the philanthropist who against all the odds inherited 31,000 acres, felt compelled to share his lands.

There were few conditions. Visitors were not charged at any of the attractions, which were open to the public every day of the year, but they were expected to sign a visitors' book. A single name would suffice for big parties. The band of the 1st Wiltshire Rifle Volunteers played in the Larmer Grounds every Sunday through the summer months.

The Larmer Grounds offered accommodation for 20 horses in its stables. 'Cyclists from all parts' also headed to Cranborne Chase. The visitor numbers for 1899 had risen to 44,417 at the Larmer Grounds, 12,611 for the Pitt-Rivers Museum, and 12,800 at King John's House. Support facilities included the Museum Hotel at Farnham which the General had extended for the benefit of visitors to the museum. The Larmer Grounds also catered for its public:

'General Rivers provides crockery, knives and forks, and other materials for picnickers, gratis. The provisions are charged for by the caretaker at a fixed rate. The attendants will expect a slight remuneration for their trouble. No other charges allowed to be made. Two cooking stoves with cooking utensils, methylated spirits, and other necessaries, are provided by General Rivers. A kitchen has

been built, and the caretaker can now provide dinners, luncheons and teas, hot or cold, but a day's notice for hot meals is necessary. A fixed tariff has been printed and can be obtained. Chairs, tables, and dumb-waiters are also provided. The caretaker can provide milk, tea, coffee, cocoa, bread, butter, salt, pepper, mustard, lemons, potatoes, ginger-beer and mineral waters, flour, fresh eggs, and some other commodities, but for parties he should know what will be required, if possible, two days before. Liquor of all kinds must be brought, if required, by the visitors. No alcoholic liquor is allowed to be sold on the grounds, except on special occasions, when due provisions will be made. German skittles, bowls, and swings are provided in the shrubbery. Chairs, tables, and benches in sufficient number, are on the lawn and in the quarters.'

There had been no instance of drunkenness, the General continued, nor trouble of any kind during the nineteen years that the Larmer Grounds and other places had been open to the public. Two policemen attended each Sunday, however, with additional constables being present when large numbers were expected. Racing and sports took place each September but gambling and betting were discouraged.

On the other side of the great estate, the Unionist victor in the north Dorset constituency in 1910 was Major Sir Randolf Littlehales Baker (1879–1959) from Ranston, who drove FX 203 and was a close friend of the Bonds from Tyneham. At 6 feet 4.5 inches in height he was the tallest member of the House of Commons. Sir Randolf, the fourth and final baronet of Ashcombe, went on to become Lieutenant-Colonel. Twice wounded in the Great War, being awarded the Distinguished Service Order and bar, he left Parliament in 1918.

PEASANTRY

Left: *Dorset peasants at Winterborne Whitechurch, typically in smocks, with pitchfork and a pottery cider-owl* (second from left) *drawn for* The Illustrated London News *in September 1846.*

Below: *The village street at Winterborne Whitechurch, downhill from the sign of the Bell in 1846, showing crumbling thatch cottages and carters and carriers on the turnpike road between Blandford and Dorchester.*

The Digby Slate and Loan Club, gathered beneath their banner beside the Fox Inn, Holwell, in the time of landlord Henry Miles and successor Walter Fox – 'Fox of the Fox' – in 1902.

Above: *Veteran socialist George Lansbury* (centre) *unveiled the headstone in the village church to James Hammett, during centenary celebrations of the Tolpuddle Martyrs, on 31 August 1934.*

Right: *Insurance agent's sign, on a cottage wall at Nettlecombe, near Powerstock, for the Dorset Rural Insurance Society which targeted agricultural workers.*

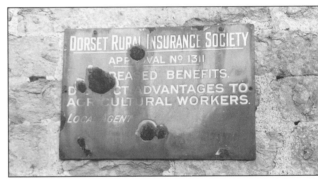

Feudalism held sway into the nineteenth century. A survey by James Bateman of *The Great Landowners of Great Britain and Ireland*, published in 1883, showed that 34 people owned 53 per cent of the land in the county of Dorset. Inevitably, there was a popular backlash, though not the revolution which the landed classes feared during the Captain Swing riots of 1830, when Charles Wollaston from Dorchester visited magistrate James Frampton at Moreton House, finding it 'barricaded like an Irish castle'.

Wages for agricultural workers were as low as a shilling a day. The reaction to such endemic poverty by the Dorset peasantry, as represented by God-fearing farm workers at Tolpuddle – Methodists to a man – took the form of a Friendly Society of Agricultural Workers. This caused disproportionate reactions throughout the judiciary, from local magistrate James Frampton and Dorchester's Lent Assize of 1834, through to Sir Robert Peel, who denounced such unions as a 'most formidable difficulty and danger' and the Home Secretary, Lord Melbourne.

Melbourne's wife, Lady Caroline Lamb, told Lady Morgan that as a child she divided the world into 'dukes and beggars' and Dorothy Marshall's biography of Lord Melbourne concedes that 'he does seem to have been oblivious to those social problems that lay outside his immediate experience'.

The result was that inappropriate laws curbing 'combinations' and 'unlawful oaths' were used against six labourers, known at the time as the 'Dorchester Unionists', which resulted in them being transported 'with indecent haste' to Australia.

Their eventual reprieve and repatriation, with a reluctantly-granted royal pardon, was due to mass meetings, petitions and protests in London. These were led by Robert Owen, whose wider efforts went into establishing a Grand National Consolidated Trades Union, and transformed the national attitude towards the Tolpuddle Martyrs. That the issue was resolved after a couple of years was due to Melbourne's rise, to Prime Minister, and his appointment of Lord John Russell to succeed him at the Home Office.

'Little Lord John,' Melbourne told King William IV, 'is utterly incapable of anything of an underhand or clandestine character'.

James Hammett, the only Tolpuddle Martyr who returned to live in the village, disclosed in 1875 that he never took part in the oath-making ceremony for which he was transported in 1834, but that he had felt compelled to withhold the true facts for personal reasons. It emerged that the Hammett who was present there and took the oath was not James but his newly-married younger brother, John, whose bride was expecting a baby.

PETS

Evelyn and Cicely Bond with tortoises beside the greenhouse at Tyneham at the turn of the twentieth century.

Cicely Bond, with Minnow the tortoise, beside the greenhouse in the walled garden of Tyneham House.

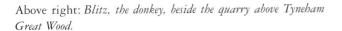

Above: *Eight-year-old Margaret Bond* (left), *with white ferret, and thirteen-year-old sister Lilian with polecat ferret Goliath, on the lawn beside Tyneham House in 1900.*

Above right: *Blitz, the donkey, beside the quarry above Tyneham Great Wood.*

Right: *Blitz requiring attention at the drawing room window of Tyneham House.*

Above: *Amos, a wire-haired terrier, on the edge of the crocus bed beside Tyneham Great Wood.*

Right: *Nancy on a chair in the grounds of Tyneham House.*

Left: *Twenty-one-year-old Lilian Bond at Lawfordshard Gate, on Whiteway Hill above Tyneham, with Amos and Grip in 1908.*

Below: *Margaret Bond (left) and sister Lilian with Dan, visiting Miss Middleton's bungalow on the cliff at Worbarrow, in 1911.*

Mrs Mary Bond with dogs Amos and Dan, and Blitz the donkey, on the lawn beside the east porch of Tyneham House, in 1912.

Dan's full name was Dan Leno, for the Victorian and Edwardian musical hall star.

Dan on Blitz in the grounds of Tyneham House.

Above: *'We all hunt in Dorset' was the caption to the photograph of this section of the field attending a meet of the Cattistock Hunt at Coryates, near Portesham, in the 1920s.*

Right: *Pet as fashion accessory, on the A357 west of the Red Lion* (top left) *at Newton, Sturminster Newton, in 1950.*

Below: *Seven-year-old Rodney Legg with his second hamster – replacing beloved Brumas – at Easter Road, Moordown, Bournemouth, in 1954.*

In the same way as my first cream-coloured hamster was called Brumas in 1952, for the polar bear born in London Zoo, Bond family pets of half a century earlier also had contemporary originals. Dan the white wire-haired terrier was officially named Dan Leno for the music hall star. Born in 1860, he was described as 'sweet looking star. Born in 1860, he was described as 'sweet looking with the saddest eyes in the whole wide world', and was not only a household name but also socially acceptable to the Tyneham gentry. This followed his command performance for the new King Edward VII, at Sandringham, in 1901. Dan Leno was the highest paid comedian in the land.

PICNICS

Above: *Six men and two ladies, freshly out of a boat, having rowed down the Stour from Wimborne to Avon Beach, Christchurch, with skipper Ernest Brett in July 1892.*

Left: *Gentlemen cliff-climbing, with the aid of a quarrymen's chain, at Dancing Ledge, Langton Matravers, in 1909.*

Arish Mell picnic in 1900 with Revd William Davy Filliter (left) and Mrs Florence Filliter beside him, and other ladies including Maud Bond, Gladys Filliter, Mrs Augustus Foster, Margaret Bond, her sister Lilian, and mother Mary Bond.

Tea at Hedbury, overlooking the English Channel between Dancing Ledge and Seacombe, in 1909.

Satisfied customers at Mrs Susan Hardy's Oak Gate tea gardens, Osmington Mills, in 1936.

Summer excursions were dominated by the needs and location of the picnic. Whatever the objective, whether it was inland, riverside or on the beach, there had to be a picnic. Such applied self-sufficiency fitted with the Puritan work ethic. Rarely were we allowed to supplement this home-made repast with open-air offerings at a tea garden.

Whether the mode of travel was car, motorcycle combination or bicycle, an objective would be selected and that was the target for the day. On arrival the ground-sheet would be produced and unfolded, a female or family task, while the leading male participant engaged in a prolonged ritual in which the Primus stove was 'pricked' and fired up with metholated spirits. The site for the picnic was required to have an open view, preferably from the privacy of a shel-

tered corner of a field, and had often been chosen many times before.

It was regarded as mindless and moronic – worthy of a disparaging remark – when others were seen to set out their picnic beside the sight, smell and sound of an arterial road.

The shot of Revd William Davy Filliter in the Arish Mell Gap, beside Worbarrow Bay, was of special significance to the son of Wareham recorder Freeland Filliter (1814–1902). Born in 1857, in St Martin's House, William Filliter married Florence Shute from Clifton, in 1883. They cherished their Purbeck days and named their home for this idyllic spot, on moving into 'Arishmel' in Powell Road, Parkstone. Their friend Mrs Augustus Foster was the widow of Lieutenant-Colonel Augustus Billett Foster of Warmwell House.

The highest point in Dorset to which a car could go, at 900 feet on Bulbarrow Hill, with a picnic party looking out over the Blackmore Vale in 1948.

PLAY

Left: *Margaret Bond and Cicely Bond at Worbarrow in 1906.*

Below: *Bonds and Blakes at South Egliston in 1906, namely Margaret Bond* (left), *Marjorie Bond, Cicely Bond, Lilian Bond on Blitz, Evelyn Blake, Phyllis Blake and Alice Blake.*

Above: *Horse collars on a troop of Blakes and Bonds featuring Cicely* (left), *Lilian, Evelyn, Alice, Winnie, Margaret, Marjorie and Phyllis.*

Right: *Comic first aid at Tyneham with victim Alice Blake* (centre), *Evelyn Blake* (left), *Winifred Blake* (with tongs), *Margaret and Lilian Bond, and Phyllis Blake* (lower right) *preparing the next case* (bottom).

Above left: *Evelyn Blake as the Queen and Lilian Bond as the King at a Warmwell House pantomime in 1909.*

Above: *Cicely Bond as the Princess and Phyllis Blake as her Prince in a pantomime at Warmwell House, the home of Mrs Augustus Foster, in 1910.*

Left: *Cicely Bond as Widow Twankey, outside the Museum at Tyneham House, in 1912.*

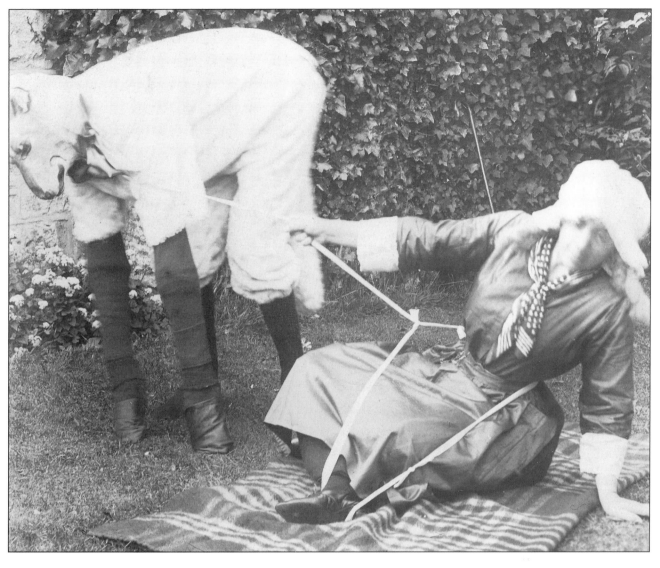

Above: *Ralph Bond as the lamb and future bride Evelyn Blake as the shepherdess in a production of 'Much Cry and Little Wool' in the barn at Tyneham Farm.*

Right: *Hilda Spencer Watson and daughter Mary (top) in the Little Theatre at their Dunshay home, Worth Matravers.*

Mary and Hilda Spencer Watson (right) *holding the stage in the Little Theatre they constructed in a barn at Dunshay, Worth Matravers.*

Play was both for indoors and out. The great divide between devising family and community entertainments and merely sitting in front of a box came with the advent of commercial television in September 1955. Things were never the same again, as I found on a Friday evening in 1964, when I walked through a street in Basildon new town and heard the synchronised strains of the 'Coronation Street' signature tune from every window. Houses in Dorset tend to be much further apart, so it was not something I had experienced before.

Prior to ITV, BBC television never had the same impact, and the wireless struggled to retain primacy with an horrific fire in an episode of 'The Archers' which has been remembered for half a century. Summers were for outdoor exploration but once the clocks were put back an hour it was an almost constant round of bridge and whist, or even beetle drives (a dice and drawing game, not involving insects), draughts and chess, theatre and cinema, pantomine and parties.

PLOUGHING

Oxen team as kept by Henry Kent at Parsonage Farm, Dewlish, seen in 1907, with Frederick Moxham (near right) *and Samuel Samways* (far right) *manoeuvring the plough.*

One man horse-plough at Langton Matravers in 1909.

Above: *Steam ploughing revived and re-enacted for the Great Dorset Steam Fair at Stourpaine Bushes in the mid-1970s.*

Left: *Plough* (centre) *between stationary steam engines* (top and foreground) *pulled by steel cables at Stourpaine Bushes.*

Opposite: *Plough seat* (top) *and blade* (left foreground), *in a cloud of steam, as heavy metal is prepared for turning at Stourpaine Bushes.*

Hoeing at Abbotsbury in 1921.

The first experimental tractor, called the 'Automobile Plough', was produced by Henry Ford in 1907. This was ten years before the first mass-market models left the production line. Ford, a farmer's son had long resented the slowness and labour-wasting methods of the horse plough. 'Why feed the power unit when it isn't working?' he asked

Not only horses furrowed Dorset fields during the opening decade of the twentieth century. Heavy steam traction engines, based at Fordington, Dorchester, worked in pairs. As they were stationary, one on either side of a field, a massive plough was towed along a cable running between them

Yet when Ford developed his tractor, he was probably unaware that in a remote English backwater oxen were still tilling the soil as they had for centuries. This primitive farming method lingered up to the Great War at Dewlish. I heard about them in 1968 from villagers at the Royal Oak Inn.

William Cross, aged eighty, remembered the teams on Parsonage Farm. 'It was a sight to see,' he told me in one of my first interviews for *Dorset – the county magazine*. Horses were used as well, and the oxen had only a second-ary role, because they could not work through the summer heat: 'They are different than what a horse is. Oxen could-n't stick the heat the same as a horse; they used to turn 'em out to grass down Tincleton way. They were down there for several months.'

In the winter the oxen were stabled, like cows, in a barn on the farm. Apart from their main work of ploughing, they occasionally hauled carts. As with horses, each of the eight oxen had its name, two being Captain and Noble. The oxen, however, were not as pleasant to handle as the hoses – 'not so clean for one thing!'

William Cross also recalled the steam ploughs, hired from the Edison Works at Fordington, to break-up the land after harvest:

'We worked with they on the farms. When I was a carter boy we hauled water and coal to where they been working. Now the trac-tors have got rid of horses and all the lot. They used to cry the trac-tors down; they didn't think anything could replace the horses. But still they do a lot quicker work than what the horses do. It was the old carters and that who didn't want to see their horses go. They were very proud and fond of them.'

POST

Vertical slit on a Victorian post-box, the oldest still in daily use in the British Isles, at Barnes Cross between Holwell and Bishops Caundle.

Post-mistress Mrs Dowland (centre) *between the bow-windows of the Post Office in West Street, Bere Regis, with her assistant Miss Eliza Lane and a boy posting a letter, in 1880.*

Morecombelake Post Office, on the corner of Pitman's Lane (left) *and Love's Lane* (right) *below the slopes of Hardown Hill, in the 1890s.*

The Post Office Stores at Colehill, facing Lonnen Road (right) *and Middlehill Road* (centre), *in the time of sub-postmaster Frank Barrett, in 1914.*

The concept of the people's post came about after 1840, not only because one could send a letter for a penny, but because a sending charge had replaced a collection fee. That system of postage due, with payment having to be made at the end of the line, must have taken much of the pleasure out of receiving messages. The post came of age in the hands of so-far failed novelist Anthony Trollope (1815–82) who devoted himself instead to an inspection of postal deliveries in rural parts of south-west England. As a result, he found himself wandering through the Close beside Salisbury Cathedral, one midsummer evening, and came up with the idea for *The Warden* which changed his fortunes in 1855.

Credited with having designed the postbox as we know it today, Trollope took a pride in widening the coverage of the postal system: 'During two years it was the ambition of my life to cover the country with rural letter carriers.'

Those days in Wiltshire, Somerset and Dorset also provided him with the characters and material that were woven into his 'Barchester' novels. He also found himself in conflict with a burgeoning bureaucracy – that of Sir Rowland Hill's Post Office – and moved these adversarial experiences sideways, disguised as fiction, into the context of the Church establishment.

Appropriately, Britain oldest working postbox is at Barnes Cross, in the Blackmore Vale. It stands beside an isolated cottage at the junction of roads from Holwell, Bishop's Caundle, King's Stag and Glanvilles Wootton. The octagonal cast-iron 'Post Office Letterbox' was made by John N. Butt & Co of Gloucester between 1853 and 1856. It would never have been intended for such a bucolic location, however, as its original position would have been somewhere prestigious, probably in Bristol.

The box is about five feet high, and each angle of the eight sides is fluted, which gives a distinctive appearance. The slot for letters is very small, being less than an inch wide and 5.5 inches deep, and is set vertically instead of being horizontal. A swinging flap, on the inside of the opening, keeps out the rain.

As well as its maker's name, the box also carries that of G.H. Gresswell, who was the Post Office's surveyor for the Western District of England. Six similar fluted boxes survive elsewhere in the country, but only that at Barnes Cross dates back to the time of the Crimean War, and must have been a prototype.

POTTERS

Left: *Puddling the clay at Verwood, with Len Sims treading barefoot, the stick giving support against slipping, and George Brewer shovelling clay* (left) *at Cross Roads Pottery, Verwood, in 1926.*

Below: *Herbert Bailey throwing a large flower-pot at Cross Roads Pottery, Verwood, with the wheel being turned by Harold Churchill with a hand-treadle* (left), *in 1927.*

Throwing a bushel-pan at Verwood, showing the wheel being turned by a hand-treadle (centre) *and some pots produced earlier* (foreground).

Left: *Herbert Fry adding handles to vases at Cross Roads Pottery, Verwood, in 1930..*

Below: *Emptying the kiln after a firing.*

Herbert Bailey throwing a jug (top left) *and Mesheck Sims a bread-bin* (right) *in a demonstration at Cross Roads Pottery, Verwood, for the photographer from* The Graphic *in 1926.*

Frederick C. W. Fry's display of his wares from Cross Roads Pottery, at Cranborne village fête, in 1909.

Rustic pottery from Verwood was hawked around the countryside, into the 1920s, by Pans Brewer.

Dorset's brief heyday in the potting industry, producing functional wheel-turned black burnished ware from kilns around Poole Harbour, was in the second half of the second century AD. That was for the Roman Army, with regular shipments to the Tyne, for garrisons on Hadrian's Wall.

Thereafter Dorset has been a backwater in potting terms, though clay-digging was revived in the eighteenth century to send top quality ball clay to the Staffordshire kilns, rather than originating fashionable products. If anything, Dorset talents regressed, to the continuing production of mediaeval designs and methods, in the guise of cheap and cheerful country pottery which was still being made and produced in the traditional way.

Costrel flagons became known as Dorset owls, slung on a leather thong for carrying cider into the fields, and occasionally doubled as the football on the village green, as recorded in at least one Thomas Hardy story. This familiar biscuit-tinted ware was also used for bed-pans, bread-pans, bushel-pans, flower vases, jugs, piggy-banks, posy-rings and potties. The yellow glaze had its roots in history, becoming doubly illegal in this controlled age, as its active ingredients included lead and urine.

POULTRY

Every farm and cottage had its chicken, for both eggs and fowl, and during the Second World War the pens spread through suburban gardens. Even a decade later, after austerity and rationing had continued until the coronation, redundant and retired old hens survived as pensioners in many town gardens.

Life and death in the poultry yard included the occasional summary execution after which I have seen at least one headless bird head off on automatic pilot down the garden path. That it knew the way so well was proof of a free-range upbringing. For this child, it was a practical demonstration of the fact that the central nervous system operates independently of the brain, for a very short time as least.

Rooster on guard in the chicken run at Tyneham, circa 1905.

Chicken feeding at Newton, Sturminster Newton, in 1948.

Quarryman Charles Hooper at Worth Matravers.

Left: *Chipping stone on the bench (centre)* in 'quarr' sheds of an *inland stone mine at Langton Matravers, in 1909.*

Below: *Capstan (near left) and its spack, having been pulled around by the donkey, to raise the cart and stone (right) up the slide in Bower's Quarry, Langton Matravers, in 1909.*

Bottom: *Older operators of Bower's Quarry, with the donkey attached to the spack, showing how stone was attached to the cart (right) to raise it from underground.*

Left: *Stone wagon of Burt and Burt from Swanage, loaded with a huge boulder, at Seacombe Quarry, Worth Matravers, in 1909.*

Below: *Team of seven horses hauling stone up Seacombe Bottom towards the Priest's Way in 1909.*

Quarry house at Winspit on the Purbeck coast.

Above: *Tripodal quarry derrick (centre foreground), at Dancing Ledge, looking east across the cliffside workings to Swanage in 1909.*

Right: *Hauling a worked stone on a trolley at Dancing Ledge in 1909.*

Below: *Sledge-hauled block being prepared for lowering, by derrick (top right), on to a Swanage-bound boat at Dancing Ledge in 1909.*

Busy time around the derrick at Dancing Ledge with blocks number 250 and 251 of a substantial order (left) *plus a great pile of random rubble* (background) *awaiting shipment in 1909.*

Ship from Swanage and its barge moored offshore as stone is prepared on Dancing Ledge for consignment in 1909.

Tons of stone already loaded, with another block in suspension (centre), *as the barge sits between rock-pools and caverns below the western end of Dancing Ledge in 1909.*

Hedbury Quarry, Langton Matravers, with a cantilever derrick (left) *from a painting by H.F. Wells in the time of Chinchen Lander, about 1865.*

Quarrying in Dorset has two historic hubs. Mediaeval Purbeck produced shelly marble, cut and polished into a dark grey finish, for effete effigies and cathedral columns across the land. Portland's more easily worked white limestone then took over, at the heart of Empire, from Sir Christopher Wren's St Paul's Cathedral to Sir Edwin Lutyens's Cenotaph in Whitehall. The Purbeck-Portland beds are geologically adjoining layers of the same warm-sea depositions along the Jurassic coast of modern day World Heritage Site designation.

Into recent times the cliff galleries of the stone plateau of the Isle of Purbeck produced high quality stone from workings at Winspit, Seacombe, Hedbury, Dancing Ledge and Tilly Whim Caves. Winspit and Tilly's Whim (as it was) took their names from the 'whim' or derrick on which squared boulders were lowered into boats, standing immediately offshore, for transit to Swanage and then larger stone boats onward to London. Seacombe is an easier place name, being the wide, deep combe that opens on to the English Channel, southwards from Eastington, between Worth Matravers and Langton Matravers. Nearby, Hedbury Quarry was named for its first operator, Thomas Eidbury. Dancing Ledge is romantically descriptive – for the sea can dance across a wide rocky pavement.

Seawards glimpse of the capstan (left) *and derrick at Hedbury Quarry, no longer in regular operation, in 1909.*

ROYALTY

King Edward VII (centre) *and his host, Lady Alington* (centre right)*, on a visit to Crichel in 1906.*

'The Sailor King' George V (centre) *arrives at Weymouth Quay, during a visit to review the Fleet, on 11 May 1912.*

Opposite: *Channel firing observed by King George V* (left) *from the foredeck of HMS* Orion *off Portland in May 1912.*

The future King Edward VIII, as Prince of Wales, with water in the wine glass as he contemplates life from Upwey Wishing Well in 1923.

Medal-bedecked Lord Lieutenant introducing a Naval welcome to Weymouth Quay for Queen Elizabeth II and Prince Charles on 29 April 1959.

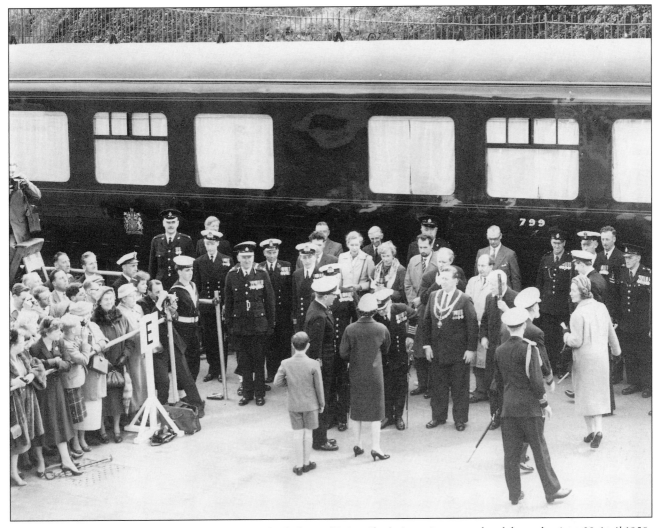

Civic and Naval farewell at Portland Dockyard as Queen Elizabeth II and Prince Charles (centre) *prepare to board the royal train on 29 April 1959.*

Generations of the royal family have come to Crichel House and Cranborne Manor for rest and recuperation. Before that, George IV found his morganatic wife at Lulworth, George III adopted Weymouth, King John hunted in Purbeck, and King Alfred ousted the Danes from the making of England by gathering resistance at Egbert's Stone, now known as Three Counties Stone, near Bourton.

Even as Prince of Wales, King Edward VII was no stranger to Dorset, having first come to Bournemouth on a walking tour as a teenager and returned to buy Lillie Langtry a love-nest in Derby Road. There was also a traditional task, to review the Fleet at Portland, though for every official visit there were several private ones for parties, shooting and occasional liaisons. Old Dorset was the equivalent of new Gloucestershire.

SHEEP

Two ewes on limestone grassland at Acton in 1909.

Three thousand sheep being herded along the Priest's Way, near Langton Matravers, in 1909.

Sheep shearing at Upwey in 1909.

Dorset horn flock, en route along Maumbury Road from Dorchester Market to the Dorset Downs, in 1938.

Mrs Ricketts and a hand-reared sheep at Sturminster Newton in 1947.

Joe Bryant, who farmed 600 acres at Berwick, near Swyre, quit sheep in 1947. He sold his prize flock of Dorset Horns, saying 'they were no longer paying their way', but always regretted losing them. He felt that all farms needed their sheep.

Berwick had been worked on a traditional four-year Dorset system of crop rotation. Clover would give the ground a rest and a boost by fixing nitrates (feeding the sheep with the land being fertilised by them). Winter wheat or barley followed. Roots were next (supporting the sheep which again fertilised the ground). Dredge corn then completed the cycle. Such had been the sequence since Bryant arrived in 1918 when Shepherd Burt was in control, 'living for his sheep'.

Almost every parish had it 'Shep'. Bincombe's shepherd, in 1950, was Ted Riglar, working for Charles Foot at East Farm. He started work at the age of twelve, a mile away at Preston Farm, and had not missed a lambing season since he began shepherding in 1901. Having sheared his first sheep at the age of fourteen, he entered a shearing competition at the Bath and West Show, when it was held at Dorchester, in 1908. There were 15 competitors and all the others had been prizewinners in lesser shows. To their astonishment, Ted won the first prize, which was £4. He married at the start of the Great War and achieved his instructor's certificate in 1918.

Starting work at five o'clock in the evening, he would set off up the steep hillside with his sheepdog, Rex. His clock was set by the trains coming and going on the railway into Weymouth. His leisure time was a half-day off which he usually spent in Weymouth.

Ernest Lovell was another 'Shep'. Born in 1891, he became a shepherd at the age of thirteen, and by the mid-twentieth century was tending the 400-strong Dorset Horn flock belonging to Maurice Tory at South Farm, Spetisbury. 'Yo' was his favourite ewe, having won ten prizes at agricultural shows, among a total of 104 awards between 1946 and 1949, including the championship at the Royal Agricultural Show for three years in succession. Lambing started in the first week of October and continued until the end of the year.

'Shep' Lovell took a particular interest in producing rams for breeding and was particularly proud of having put 34 animals, at Croydon Aerodrome in 1947, for export to Italy. He lamented having no son to follow him and was pessimistic about the chances of the post-war generation taking up shepherding:

'Young chaps want to go to football on Saturdays, and this is a seven days a week job.'

So it was until the advent of modern farming. Wartime ploughing started the process which resulted in the historic sheep leazes turning into fields of grain. The big flocks melted from the Dorset Downs like a winter snow, initially retreating into the valleys and vales, and are now almost an endangered species.

SHOOTING

Ralph Bond (right foreground), *squire of Tyneham and an international top-shot, with the Long family and friends from Cheshire and North Yorkshire, in 1905.*

Edwardian gentlemen, nicknamed in the caption as 'Cocky' Melegan (left), 'Lucy' Long, and 'Gladys' (Ralph) Bond, on a shooting and fishing visit to Ranston.

Hooray Henries mustering two walking sticks, one shotgun, a magnifying glass and a rifle beside the quarry shed at Winspit in 1909.

Telescopic appraisal (left) of coastal gunnery at Winspit in 1909.

Dorset's game birds were partridge, pheasant and waterfowl. Rabbits hardly qualified, to gentlemen, and wild deer have only established themselves in substantial numbers in recent decades. Socially acceptable prey species tended to be upstaged by grouse on the northern moors and big game in Africa. Shooting for pleasure was never quite the same after service on the Western Front.

SNOW

Salisbury Street, Shaftesbury, in the cold winter of 1886.

The 'Snow Elephant' on the lawn beside Tyneham House, looking east into the avenue, in 1899.

Dan (centre left) *and Amos in the Eweleaze, looking west to Tyneham Farm and Flower's Barrow, on 8 March 1916.*

The road between Gallows Gore and Langton Matravers, looking east with Worth Matravers signed on the right, from the 'eight mile stone' (from Wareham) in 1924.

Concrete blocks (right) stacked ready for building work, beside half-timbered cottages opposite the Red Lion at Newton, Sturminster Newton, in the cold winter of 1947.

Summer and winter contrasts in 1946-47 up Kempston Road, Weymouth, from No. 18 Rodwell Avenue to Bincleaves Plantation.

Deep drifts in the lane between New Cross and Hammoon in February 1947.

Snowballing at Sturminster Newton in 1947.

Venturing into the oaks of Piddles Wood, between Sturminster Common and Fiddleford, in the winter of 1947.

Goods train being pulled by Somerset and Dorset Railway locomotive No. 53808, southwards across the Mendip Hills, in February 1956.

The junction of the Broadmayne road on Ridgeway Hill, above Weymouth, four weeks into the big freeze on 19 January 1963.

The A35 westbound from Rew towards the Roman Road (centre background) *on 25 January 1963.*

Iron Age ramparts and sheep walks on the southern slopes of Maiden Castle, etched in snow, on 17 January 1963.

These days, whenever there is a scatter of snow, older people make comparisons with the deep-frozen snow and intense cold that went on for months during the winter of 1962–63. Similarly, my parents used to mention the prolonged cold of a post-war winter, after which I emerged as a spring birth, on 18 April 1947. Then, my father would add, the railways were bankrupt, coal was in short supply, and there were regular power cuts.

To my grandfather's generation, the memories centred on the 'great winters' of the 1880s and 1890s. Those decades started with a blizzard which had cut off all roads in Dorset by 20 January 1881. For the previous three days and nights, the county had endured strong northerly winds, which drove snow into every crevice of buildings and piled it in the lanes until it was level with the tops of hedgerows. Only the railways continued to function and one of the more fortune of the otherwise cut-off communities was Bradford Abbas where a wagon and coal was emptied down the embankment for the benefit of villagers.

Ice, however, brought recreational possibilities. By 19 December 1890 there was a sufficient thickness across Sherborne Lake to draw hundreds of skaters from miles around:

'Some are accomplished, others amateurish. They are being joined by hundreds of promenaders and people of all ages who are indulging in the old fashioned pastime of sliding. Some have come to grief, but so far no one has experienced worse than a cold bath.'

Others ran out of luck that winter. On 9 March 1891, when all roads in Dorset were blocked by deep snow, there was a report of a man being lost in the blizzard, somewhere between Maiden Newton and Sydling St Nicholas. Searchers recovered the body of John Guppy, near Sydling, and PC James Searley notified the coroner.

Another fall of intensely fine powdery snow, carried by a gale which reached storm force 10 during the night, blanketed the West Country in the early hours of Tuesday 11 March 1891. Huge drifts cut off the South-West peninsula. Those between Lyme Regis and Honiton were 20 feet high, making it impossible to find the main road, and the sub-zero temperature felt even colder in the strong winds:

'On the Sunday following the blizzard the body of a man named Bisgood, a labourer, was found near Offwell. He had not been seen alive after leaving the New Inn, Honiton Hill, on Tuesday evening.'

TREES

The Remedy Oak, at Sutton Holms, near Wimborne St Giles, where King Edward VI 'touched for the King's Evil'.

Above: *The Posy Tree, a sycamore beside Corpse Lane at Mapperton, in 1974.*

Right: *'In September 1666, the Great Plague reached its peak and at this point Mapperton survivors gathered with herbs and flowers to ward off the plague as the bodies of the dead were taken up this lane to a common grave.'*

Oak trees Gog (left) and Magog (right) at Somerset Gate, Glanvilles Wootton, marking what used to be the county boundary when the adjoining parish of Holwell was a detached part of Somerset.

Right: *Winter study of an English elm, common in hedgerows but scarce as a specimen tree, at Hurn in 1925.*

Below: *Borough of Weymouth tree surgeons removing stricken elms in 1975.*

Rare black poplar with mistletoe on Bottlebush Down, Wimborne St Giles, late coming into leaf when Edwin Dodshon photographed it, on 16 May 1925.

Trees endure, at least for half a millennium in special cases, to mark boundaries or carry the folk memory of what is still living history both to the community and the plant. The national tree, the oak, is well represented in both. A huge, hollow and now topless tree at Silton, Wyndham's Oak has a girth of 35 feet and is named for Sir Hugh Wyndham (1603–84), a Baron of the Exchequer and the great survivor of circuit judges who served both Charles I and the Commonwealth.

Wyndham had no problem with whether his face fitted the new regime. For Dorothy Cromwell. wife of Lord Protector Richard Cromwell, was born Dorothy Major – the daughter of the lord of the manor of Silton – and had sat at the judge's feet under the famous tree.

For height it is upstaged by the Stockbridge Oak, opposite the Holm Bushes at Lillington, and by Gog and Magog between Glanvilles Wootton and Holwell.

The Remedy Oak, in the parish of Wimborne St Giles, stands on the roadside edge of King's Wood and faces Remedy Gate Cottage. Its block of dense woodland, opposite Sutton Common, is 2 miles west of Verwood. A plaque reads:

'According to tradition, King Edward VI sat beneath this tree and touched for the King's Evil, circa 1552.'

The disease was scrofula, a tuberculosis of the lymph glands, which caused painful and unsightly swellings, and was thought to be curable by a King's touch. By the mid seventeenth century such beliefs were institutionalised and in 1684 John Browne, 'Chirurgeon in Ordinary to His Majesty', published *Charisma Basilicon, or, The Royal Gift of Healing Strumaes or King's Evil* in which he showed from registers kept by members of the royal household that 92,000 had been touched for the disease between 1660 and 1682.

Remedy Oak preserves the memory of an unknown unfortunate who begged the royal touch when the King passed through Dorset, probably en route to Cranborne Manor. It has a massive hollow trunk but still supports a healthy crown and a heavy crop of acorns.

On the other hand, another historic tree was dying at the turn of the new millennium, far away in the western hills. The Posy Tree at Mapperton was a sycamore which took its name from the 'Ring of Roses' tradition that is also commemorated by a public house at Holcombe, near Bath. Posies of roses were thought to ward off the plague.

Corpse Lane at Mapperton, a green road north-westwards from the village, used to be known as Dead Man's Lane. Mapperton was only a small community, of under a hundred souls, and its dead were carried along the stony track, downhill to neighbouring Netherbury, for burial. In the seventeenth century, however, the dreaded disease was the plague – known to be contagious – and the men of Netherbury came 'armed with staves' to prevent the first cortege with its victims from entering their parish.

There was a fight, on Warren Hill, and Mapperton people were forced to dig a plague pit – since marked by conifers – for their dead. Perhaps 1666, the date on the sycamore's plague plaque, was not the year of the skirmish. There is a record that Mapperton churchwardens John Mondayn and John Ford, with sidesmen John Roper and Oliver Modeyne, registered a complaint 'that the vicar of Netherbury doth deny to bury the dead of the parish of Mapperton' or 'suffer his curate to do it'.

Nico Barrington's research also showed that the year of the Great Plague in London, 1665 as the precursor to the Great Fire, was without apparent incident or an abnormal number of local deaths. It seems instead to have been a settled period as Richard Broadrepp built a dovecote at Mapperton Manor which carries a 1665 date-stone.

The plaque date came from county historian John Hutchins who stated in 1783 that 'the tenants all dying of the plague in 1666, all houses in Coltley [Coltleigh] and Mapperton fell into the lord's hands, and were pulled down'. Traces of foundations, house platforms and closes can be seen to the north of the manor house, beside the lane over Storridge Hill.

Past accounts of the story have assumed that the now deceased sycamore was the successor of the first Posy Tree but in 1976, A.W.J. Cobham of Beaminster provided me with evidence that it was in fact the original. Sycamores three centuries old are on record, he pointed out:

'The Mapperton tree is 13 feet in circumference and is now about 32 feet high. At some time in its history it was struck by lightening and broken off about ten feet from the ground; at the same time it must have been set on fire as the whole of the inside of the tree was burnt out. This was revealed when I pushed a camera and flashgun through a small hole at ground level.'

An amateur woodsman, namely the Revd Claude Homan, who was rector of Tyneham from 1897 to 1917.

Gentleman with shotgun (right) and hurdle-maker in what was described as 'wicket fence making' at Witchampton in 1903.

Stephen Steel's billhook slicing a hazel rod into two split gads, at Woodcutts, in 1971.

A garden hurdle nearing completion.

Fitting the spur which is the last of the top-binders.

I found my archetypal woodsman in a clearing he had created himself in the woods of Woodcutts at the heart of the Pitt-Rivers Estate near Sixpenny Handley. When Stephen Steel started work as a hurdle-maker in the coppices of Cranborne Chase he was one of more than thirty workers. By the summer of 1970–71 there were only six and no young men were taking up the job. It was a time before grants and subsidies for the management of woods for wildlife purposes. The acreage of suitable woods was declining each year.

Stephen Steel was living at Farnham on the edge of the widest expanse of ancient woodland in Dorset. Since 1950 he had worked full-time in a craft that can never be modernised. There was a hope that a chain-saw would help but the technology available at the time was beaten and broken by the brushwood. Mr Steel wished to employ someone to cut the wood for him, but there were no part-timers left, and the contemporary generation of old age pensioners required trade union rates before they would pick up a saw.

So he was working alone, with a curved billhook of solid steel, and deftly spliced every rod without anyone to notice. Once he was joined by his son, 'he was a good quick hurdler, but you can't keep the youngsters to it – there's no future'.

These was also little money and constant problems in the hiring of tractors and lorries that have to penetrate deep into the woods. Output was therefore restricted and demand had also reduced. When I interviewed Stephen he was making a 6-feet garden panel. There was less call for the traditional sheep hurdle.

He could make three such garden hurdles on an average day, but conceded that 'young fellows can manage a little bit more'. The weather was crucial as it could play havoc with woodland work. Stephen travelled by motor-cycle and the main enemy was the rain, causing lost days and wasted petrol, but extreme climatic events were in another league: 'In the snow of 1963 I never done a thing for two months, the stuff was afroze a-solid'.

Hazel makes the best hurdles, I was told, when it has had fourteen to seventeen years' growth after last being coppiced. I have since learnt that such trees can live for ever, as long

as there is no break in the process and programme of coppicing, as has been proved by the examination of woods that have been cut from Saxon times to the present day.

On the other hand the woodsmen have to work with what they have, and that at Woodcutts was obviously a lot younger and it had become a messy patch of scrub with birch, blackthorn and brambles as well. In the past the hazel had grown up under a canopy of oak trees but now, once it was cleared, there would be no more coppicing as conifers were to be planted.

The cost of buying a perch (otherwise known as a pole, measuring 30.25 square yards) was an old-value penny in 1950. By 1951 it had risen to 15p in new money for poorer wood. Extrapolated to costs for an acreage, there are 40 poles to the rood, and four roods to the acre. That puts the price per acre at £3-6s.-8d. in 1950; rising to £60 in 1970. Costs and other difficulties had brought the craft to the brink of unprofitability, but land and house values continued to push up the price of fencing, and demand remained healthy.

Dorset's 'Chase-type' pattern of hurdle-making had its own language and even a Hampshire hurdle-maker might scratch his head on hearing the dialect words even if both made identical products.

A cut length of hazel is known as a 'rod'. Once the billhook has been sliced through it becomes 'split gads'. The hurdle is assembled on a 'lathe'. This is a block of curved birch wood with a flat upper surface. The convex curve produces tension on the hurdle so that when it is completed and removed it springs out straight and rigid.

The lathe is fastened to the ground and bored with nine round holes. Into each of these holes go upright rods which are called 'sails'. A few rods of hazel and then ash are used to bind the base and then the split gads are added.

Special skill is needed to complete the top of the hurdle. Imagine you are looking at a hurdle on the lathe, with both of them curving outwards, away from you. There are three key top-binders that will hold the hurdle together. 'Stumpy', at the right-hand corner, holds the 'finisher'. The latter is a double-twist. Stumpy is the Dorset word for short and thick. Its purpose is to stop the finisher from loosening and lifting as the hurdle dries out.

The third and final top-binder is the 'spur' at the left end which is doubled back at an angle. This pressure keeps the top in place. Then the ends and sides of the hurdle are trimmed with a 'nobbin hook', which for the past half century has come into the category of a bygone instrument, of the sort that has to be acquired second-hand at an agricultural fair rather than from a manufacturer.

The difference between a garden hurdle and a sheep hurdle is one sail. A garden hurdle has nine sails whereas a sheep hurdle of the same length has ten. This makes the sheep hurdle more sturdy, and therefore durable, as it has to be moved around.

Wildlife provided company for Stephen Steel but the deer were among life's lesser problems. They sometimes rubbed the wood and made it useless for anything other than bean sticks. The damage occurs when the deer is casting its coat or a buck cleaning velvet from its antlers.

Since the early 1960s, as a result of the Space programme developing solid-state transistors, there was also a radio for company. This, I heard, was to break the monotony rather than for listening. Not having workmates was compounded by seldom seeing a keeper. Just one hurdle-maker and a reporter who had come across him. There was, however, a third person in the middle of the wood that day in 1971.

Walking there I had passed a woman who was stacking neatly-cut lengths of wood on to a cart. This had to be hauled for 2 miles along muddy and rutted tracks that led back to her cottage. Other villagers had said she would never manage such an effort but she could not otherwise afford to keep her home comfortably warm. The wood she was loading had been cut and left there for her to collect by our kindly hurdle-maker.

Stacks of finished garden hurdles and a trolley of logs (left) *beside a forest track at Woodcutts, Sixpenny Handley, in the winter of 1970–71.*